Samuel Ireland

Picturesque views on the upper, or Warwickshire Avon

Samuel Ireland

Picturesque views on the upper, or Warwickshire Avon

ISBN/EAN: 9783742827036

Manufactured in Europe, USA, Canada, Australia, Japa

Cover: Foto ©Andreas Hilbeck / pixelio.de

Manufactured and distributed by brebook publishing software (www.brebook.com)

Samuel Ireland

Picturesque views on the upper, or Warwickshire Avon

PICTURESQUE VIEWS

ON

THE UPPER, OR WARWICKSHIRE

AVON.

PICTURESQUE VIEWS

ON THE

UPPER, OR WARWICKSHIRE

AVON,

FROM ITS SOURCE AT NASEBY TO
ITS JUNCTION WITH THE

SEVERN AT TEWKESBURY:

WITH

OBSERVATIONS

ON

THE PUBLIC BUILDINGS,

AND

OTHER WORKS OF ART IN ITS VICINITY.

BY SAMUEL IRELAND,

Author of " A Picturesque Tour through Holland, Brabant, and
Part of France;" and of
" Picturesque Views on the Rivers Thames, Medway," &c.

London:

PUBLISHED BY R. FAULDER, NEW BOND STREET;
AND T. EGERTON, WHITEHALL.

1795.

TO

THE EARL OF WARWICK.

My Lord,

THE very flattering approbation I received from your Lordship in the course of the present undertaking, has been no small incitement to my labours, and has induced me to pursue with confidence and alacrity, a work, in which the good opinion

opinion of persons of true taste has ever been my first aim, and its attainment the completion of my wishes.

The exalted rank your Lordship justly holds in society, and the conspicuous, venerable, and dignified mansion you so truly enjoy on the bank of that Avon, which forms so leading a feature in its embellishments, would naturally suggest a wish to find in such a place protection and patronage: yet these circumstances, flattering as they are, were not the principal inducement to affix your name to this work.

THE knowledge and taste you have displayed, both in the works of your own pencil, as well as the selection of those of the first masters in the different schools of painting, give you a superior claim in appretiating the merits of others: and more especially of a work like this, in which the contemplation of the beautiful scenery of our country, and an invariable attention to every production in the fine arts, with which it is enriched, form the principal and leading features. Presuming, therefore, in some degree, upon your Lordship's approbation of this volume, I venture to lay it before the Public,

and

and to subscribe myself, with all due respect,

My Lord,

Your Lordship's very obliged

and obedient Servant,

Sam^L. Ireland.

Norfolk Street,
Strand,
May 7, 1795.

PREFACE.

THE Upper or Warwickſhire Avon, though not equally famed for the nature and extent of its commerce, as for the many beautiful and elegant ſcenes diſplayed on its banks, yet deſervedly holds a pre-eminent rank amongſt the leſſer rivers, that ſo abundantly fertilize our luxuriant iſland. Had the vicinity of our Avon in its gentle and meandering courſe exhibited leſs of the picturesque, or of the magnificent fragments of antiquity, than it can in ſo many inſtances juſtly boaſt, yet ſtill, the honour it derives from having produced our immortal

tal Shakſpeare, "ſo divine in reaſon! and "in faculties ſo infinite, the paragon of "the world!" would alone have been ſufficient to induce the author to have aſpired at being its hiſtorian.

If in the pages of this volume he may be thought in the ſmalleſt degree to have elucidated any circumſtance of Shakſpeare's life, or any paſſage in the noble effuſions of his more than human mind, his utmoſt pride and wiſh is fully gratified; and the author can truly affirm, that long ſince he had committed this expreſſion of his feelings to paper, he has had the ſingular felicity of obtaining a treaſure, which had not rewarded the reſearches of thoſe who have been moſt aſſiduous and active in tracing the ſources of our earlieſt literature.

To

To this pursuit he has not himself been indifferent; yet neither to the present moment had his own enquiries been completely successful: He may say,

> "Quod optanti Divûm promittere nemo
> "Auderet, volvenda dies en attulit ultro."
>
> *Æn.* 9. 6.

It is enough to add that he has the means, and it is his intention, so soon as opportunity shall serve, to lay before the public a variety of authentic and important documents respecting the private and public life of this wonderful man: one of his most affecting and admired Tragedies, written with his own hand, and differing in various particulars of much curiosity and interest from any edition of that work now extant; and at a future day to present a picture

picture of that mind, which no one has yet ever presumed to copy, an entire Drama! yet unknown to the world, in his own hand-writing. This general information on a subject that, it is presumed, cannot but prove acceptable to every reader of taste and refinement, the author feels it a duty here to disclose, as it is nearly connected with the intention of the present undertaking —a History of that river on whose banks nature has in a happy and propitious hour teemed forth her proudest work.

To explore this gentle river, together with the various others so greatly conducive to the health and fertility of our island; to delineate their many picturesque beauties, and to become (however unworthily) their historian, had very early been the

the favourite object, and has for several years been the avowed purpose, of the author of this work: in this aim he has so far succeeded as to have received the approbation of a liberal public, testified in the course of this pursuit by a rapid demand of his publications. The idea of becoming their historian, which originated with the author, and which he conceived with a view to his amusement alone, has proved, in its progress, a source of the most rational pleasure and improvement.

The mind, thus occupied, receives its gratifications without alloy, while new images and unthought of views of things present and impress themselves, and fatigue is lost in the double satisfaction arising from the

en-

enjoyment of the scene before him, and the reflections that are suggested by it.

The drawings for this work were all made by the author in the summer months of 1792 and 1793; in these he professes to give real portraits, without sacrificing truth to effect, or striving to give to nature those fanciful, adscititious ornaments, which so often load and encumber her, and which so rarely grace, or sit easy upon her natural shape. In that light may be considered the many elegant essays, with which the refined ear of the public has of late been so much fascinated on the subject of the picturesque and beautiful: these, how high soever their claim to merit, whatever superiority may be discovered in the style and taste of their com-

composition, may yet be considered as little more than efforts of imagination, and works of ingenious speculation. Nature still holds her original forms, the grand, and majestic! the smooth, and the placid! and these all wisely contrasted by her hand, generally produce in effect, that happy assemblage of parts, which rarely fails to act upon the mind, like the judicious combination of light and shade, in a well composed picture. To exhibit this scenery of nature as it presented itself, the writer has considered as his primary duty; conceiving that the pencil and pen of the historian should not on any occasion be otherwise employed, than in the delineation of truth, and should rather humbly follow the great outline she has marked, than loftily prescribe the path in which she ought to have trod.

THE

PREFACE.

The writer thinks it neceſſary to inform the public, that the ſcenery of the river Wye, ſo peculiarly adapted to the pencil from its diverſified luxuriancy, will be the next ſubject laid before them, and will be followed by the Hiſtory and Picturefque Scenery of the Lower, or Bath Avon.

PRINTS

Picturesque Views

ON THE

Warwickshire Avon.

SECTION I.

THE river Avon derives its source from a spring called Avon Well, in the village of Naseby, or, as it is written in Domesday book, Navesberie, in the county of Northampton. Avon, Even, or Sevon, is a name common to rivers whose course is easy and gentle. The Avon Well is in the north-west quarter of the village, at a small distance from the market cross which stands before the church, in the midst of an area of about an acre, as defcribed in the annexed view. Nafeby is remarkable for the excellence and number of its fprings; not lefs than fix having their rife in this village. The waters, falling from the neighbouring hills, are carefully received in many places, and form fo many refervoirs for the conftant fupply of cattle in the townfhip. The lower fpring, in Nafeby, called Warrin's Well, is faid to have a flavour fo peculiarly grateful, and even an effluvia fo inviting, that cattle are with difficulty made to pafs it without ftopping to drink; and, when they have tafted it, they are more eager after it than any other water in the neighbourhood.

MORTON, in his Natural Hiftory of this county, fays, " It is a blue water, in-
" dicating a coal mine not far diftant, be-
" caufe the like waters are obferved where
" the coal delves are."

NASEBY Field gives rise to the river Nine, or Nen, at a spring called Chapel Well; which, passing Northampton, becomes navigable from thence to Wellingborough, Peterborough, &c. and falls into the sea at Lynn. The river Ise, or Isebrook, likewise rises from many springs in the north-east quarter of this field, from whence it winds its course to Kelmarsh, &c. and joins the river Nine, near Wellingborough.

This field produces another spring, called St. Dennis's Well, about a mile west of Naseby. It is remarkable for the coldness of its water in the summer months; and was formerly used as a bath by invalids in various chronic complaints, with considerable efficacy. It is now overgrown with weeds and sedges, and is no longer resorted to.

The village of Naseby stands nearly in the centre of this memorable field, which is supposed to be the highest ground in England; for the rivers Nine, and Avon, which take their rise in this field, discharge themselves into the sea, the former at Lynn, on the eastern, the latter, by the Severn, below Bristol, on the western side of the island. It is likewise said to lie in, or very near the centre of the kingdom; which conjecture is corroborated by its name, which is derived from the Saxon word Nare, or Nave, signifying a centre.

The village is pleasantly situated, and, from various points, commands several very extensive and picturesque views, in which are included near forty parish churches, which circumscribe this immense space of Naseby field. The prospects within the limits of the village wear a different aspect: indigent cottagers, and clay, or earth-built huts, are the whole it presents, and these, in number and wretchedness, are hardly to be equalled,

equalled. Naseby church is a structure of an ancient date; but at what period it was built, or who was its founder, history affords no record. The form of the tower is very singular, and strikes the stranger, at first view, as having been left unfinished, being only the half of a pyramid; but, on a close investigation, it does not appear that the architect intended it to have been carried higher; and indeed he hardly could have so done, as there does not appear a sufficient degree of massiveness or strength in the lower parts to support a complete spire of stone.

Some years ago, Mr. Ashby, lord of the manor, caused some additions, at a considerable expence, to be made to this tower; at the top of which is placed a large copper ball, which was brought from Boulogne, by Sir Gyles Allington, in the reign of king Henry the eighth, an. Dom. 1544. Its original

nal station in this island, was the cupola of Sir Gyles's house, which he built at Horseheath, in Cambridgeshire. At the demolition of this mansion, it was sold with the rest of the materials, and purchased by Mr. Ashby, as old copper. In a house in the village of Naseby, built by Mr. Ashby, I was shewn a large oak table, at which, tradition says, a party of the king's life guards were sitting down to supper, the night before the battle of Naseby, where they were surprised, and taken prisoners by Ireton, the parliament general. This tradition is corroborated by the Anglia Rediviva, published in 1647, by Joshua Sprigge, chaplain to general Fairfax, in which we find the following passage: "Tidings "were brought to the general, of the good "services done by colonel Ireton, in falling "into the enemy's quarters, which they had "newly taken up in Naseby town, where he "took many prisoners, life guards, &c. &c.

PROBABLY thefe life guards were thofe of the Prince Rupert, not the King's, as it does not appear that he ever was in the town of Nafeby. From Nafeby the river Avon winds its mazy courfe in a wefterly direction through Nafeby field towards Sulby Abbey, a diftance of about three miles. This extenfive plain, rendered famous for its many productions of rivers and falubrious fprings, is not lefs fo from the importance of the battle there fought on the 14th of July 1645, between the Parliament Army and that of Charles the Firft; whofe fate was decided by that memorable event. Nafeby field is near twenty miles in circumference, and in point of fituation is moft excellently difpofed for a field of battle. The fpot occupied by the armies was north-weft of the town, and is eafily diftinguifhed by the many hollows in which the dead were buried. The word of the day, on the fide of the parliament, was, "*God our ftrength*;" on that of the king, "*God*

"*God and queen Mary.*" The particulars of this engagement are too well known to need a recital; and although its consequences were such as to produce a total overthrow of the political system of our government, yet the effusion of blood was so little proportioned to that which has been spilt in the shock of modern civil conflicts, as to render it, comparatively, only a skirmish. Fifteen hundred are said to have been about the number slain on that day; when, as a mere prelude to conquest, in a neighbouring country, we find more than as many thousands killed in a morning. We are well informed that, in the civil commotions that at present agitate that nation, " it has already cost the " lives of near two hundred and twenty " thousand men, to stop the progress of the " war in La Vendée; a very inconsiderable " district in that country."

The graves that were dug in Naseby field, for

for the burial of the dead (an office performed by the neighbouring country people), are still visible. Several of these, from being sunk in hollows much below the general surface, we opened in the presence of the Rev. Mr. Maftyn, vicar of Naseby; they contained many human bones, as well as those of horses, and appear to have been about five or six feet deep; the soil within is of a black and unctuous quality, evidently enriched with human sacrifices.

MANY strange stories are told of the mode of burying the dead at that period, and of the credulity of the ignorant with respect to their ghosts and supposed appearance afterwards.

THE following anecdote, as applicable to the uncertain events of human life, and the hair-breadth 'scapes of battle, I received upon the spot, from the Rev. Mr. Maftyn,

Maftyn, and give it to the reader in his own words. "The late Dr. Hill, rector of Thorpe Malfon, in Northamptonfhire, brother to Serjeant Hill, informed me, that he had a relation, a Mr. Manfell, who fought in the battle of Nafeby field, that he was wounded in the breaft, and left for dead; and, being ftripped to be buried, a young woman, daughter to an apothecary, happening to be upon the field, and finding his hand to be very foft, exclaimed, This certainly was a gentleman! She farther obferved, that fhe felt a pulfe, and confequently that he was not quite dead. She put off her under petticoat, and, wrapping him in it, had him conveyed to a neighbouring village, where he recovered, and lived fome years after. He kept the young woman as a companion or houfe-keeper till the time of his death, when he left her a handfome annuity."

I CAN-

I CANNOT quit this subject without adverting to the chimerical conjecture of Oliver Cromwell's having been buried in Naseby field: " Bankes, in the account of his life, " says, that Barkstead, lieutenant of the " tower, and a great confidant of Crom- " well's, did, amongst other such confidants, " in the time of his illness, desire to know " where he would be buried? To which the " protector answered, Where he had ob- " tained the greatest victory and glory, and " as nigh the spot as could be guessed, where " the heat of action was, viz. in com. " Northamptonshire, at midnight. Soon " after his death, the body being embalmed " and wrapped in a leaden coffin, was in a " hearse conveyed to the said field, Mr. " Barkstead, the son, then about fifteen " years old, attending, by order of his " father, close to the hearse. Being come " to the field, they found, in the midst of " it, a grave dug about nine feet deep, with
" the

" the green fod carefully laid on one fide,
" and the mould on the other; in which the
" coffin being put, the grave was inftantly
" filled up, and the green fod laid exactly
" flat upon it, care being taken that the
" furplus mould fhould be clean removed.
" Soon after, the like care was taken
" that the ground fhould be ploughed up,
" and it was fowed fucceffively with corn.
" Other material circumftances," fays the
fame author, " the faid Mr. Barkftead, who
" now frequents Richards's coffee houfe,
" within Temple Bar, relates relative to this
" burial." Notwithftanding this teftimony of
Mr. Barkftead, there is no reafon to fuppofe
it is founded in truth. I took much pains to
get fome information relative to this occurrence; but could only learn, that tradition had pointed out a fpot where he was faid to have been buried; and that a curious friend of mine, in confequence of it, had dug there, and had difcovered a human
fkeleton;

skeleton: but that on a close investigation, it was found not to be the Protector, but that of a person who had been hung for a robbery near the spot, within the last century.

From Naseby the Avon winds its course, in a western direction, through part of this extensive field, towards the small remains of Sulby abbey, founded about the year 1155, by W. De Wideville, or Wevill, as a convent of the Premonstratensian order. At the time of its foundation, it was called Welford abbey. At the dissolution, the clear yearly income of this abbey appears to have been £258. 8s. 5d. In the 12th of Elizabeth, the monastery, with other demesnes, were granted to Christopher Hatton, Esq. in exchange for Holdenbey manor, which, on the death of the said Christopher, devolved to the crown. It is now a respectable farm house, and has only a few fragments

ments of old stone walls, decorated with heads of monks, &c. here and there scattered about, to indicate what was its original destination.

Like most other religious devotees, these pious recluse appear to have taken good care that their house should not want any of the comforts of wood and water; soft shade to cool the fervor of their devotion; and delicate fish to enable them to support the rigours of ecclesiastical abstinence.

SECTION II.

FROM Sulby abbey our gentle Avon, in a circuitous course, winds its way towards the village of Welford, a distance of near two miles westward. The approach to this pleasant village from the river, yields rather an agreeable landscape; an ancient stone bridge, part of the village, and the venerable tower of the church, modestly rising above the neighbouring objects, combine happily, and give that sort of view, which, being simple in itself, seldom fails to constitute elegance. The church is of very high antiquity, and is dedicated to the Virgin Mary. At the end of each aisle is a chantery chapel, and a few ancient monuments. This church, with nine carucates of land in Sulby (viz. as much land as may be tilled in a year with one plough), were given to the convent of

Sulby

Sulby by Richard de Wideville, with the consent of his superior, lord Roger de Moubray, and confirmed to it by Richard the first, and Edward the second in the ninth year of his reign. Crossing the church yard, the eye is caught by an inscription of rather a whimsical nature: it is the composition of a singular character named William Patch, who describes himself as having, after an ineffectual struggle, sunk into the grave in consequence of sympathies that have not been found, at any period of history, to have greatly thinned the human race. The efforts he made are given in the following couplet:

"She first departed, He for a little try'd
"To live without her, lik'd it not, and dy'd."

WELFORD yields little, besides its pleasing situation, to attract the stranger, or to gratify the curious enquirer. I shall therefore digress a few miles beyond the present subject of investigation toward the ancient town of Leicester;

Leicester; and flatter myself, that the motive which induced me to stray so far from the banks of the Avon, will be found to carry with it my apology to the reader.

Feeling it, as I do, an interesting duty as well as a grateful employment, to trace any thing that bears relation to the works of that immortal bard, the native of Avon's banks, I cannot forego even the slight opportunity that now offers.

The town of Leicester boasts two curious remains which must be admitted to have reference to his works: the house and bed in which Richard the third slept the night before the battle of Bosworth, or rather Sutton, field. The house, of which the adjoining sketch is a faithful representation, is known by the appellation of the Blue Boar Inn, a name probably derived from the crest of Richard, which was that of a boar. In allusion

allusion to this crest, the lord Hastings says to Catesby,

> " Stanley did dream the boar did rase our helms,
> " But I did scorn it, and disdain to fly."

The house is still in good preservation, and the room in which the king slept, is so spacious as to cover the whole premises; it is situated on the first floor, agreeable to a style of building at that time very common in most of our ancient inns.

SHAK-

SHAKSPEARE, in introducing Richard in the tent scene, has, beyond a doubt, heightened the interesting part of the tragedy, by using a poetical licence, though he has deviated from the first historical authority, from whom that inference, which is confirmed by the traditional account it obtains in the town, seems to arise. This historian, Speed, speaking of his being at Nottingham at the time the news was brought of the earl of Richmond's advance to Litchfield, says, " Hee (the king) marchelled his fol-
" lowers; and like a valiant captaine and
" politicke leader, set forward his battailes,
" five and five in a rank. In the midst of
" his troops he bestowed his carriages, and
" himself mounted upon a white courser in-
" vironed with his guard, followed by his
" footman and the wing of his horsemen,
" ranged on every side with a frowning
" countenance, but yet in great pompee, en-
" tered the town of Leicester after the sun

" was set; being full of indignation and
" swelling in anger, which somewhat he
" asswaged with threat of revenge."

The bedstead, from which the above sketch is made, is now in the possession of Mr. Alderman Drake, who purchased it for about forty shillings of one of the servants of of the forementioned Inn about twenty years ago. It is of oak, and richly carved with Gothic ornaments suitable to the taste of the time, but at what period it was made, is not clearly ascertained: though a date I am informed appeared on one of the feet, when it was last taken down, but no person had the curiosity to notice it. When purchased by Mr. Drake, much of the old gilding appeared about the ornaments. Some particulars of this bedstead I also understand are preserved in the records of the corporation.

The following brief account, is the traditional history as received on the spot; viz. That Richard, when travelling, always carried among his baggage this bedstead, which, having a false bottom, enabled him with secresy to convey his treasure unsuspected, and that he slept in it in that house the night before the battle. After the battle of Bosworth field, the bed remained in the house undis-

undisturbed till the reign of James the first, when the then owner of it, a Mr. Clarke, or his wife, by some accident discovered a very considerable treasure therein concealed. The fact remained unknown till after the death of the husband; when, as it is proverbially said of a woman, "that she cannot keep a secret," it by some means or other transpired; and whether the maid servant, by any indiscreet confidence, was made a repository of this secret, or by any accident or observation was led to the discovery, we are told that she, with the assistance of others, murdered the mistress, and plundered the house, and were for this crime all hanged at Leicester. At that period the bedstead was purchased by one of the servants of the Inn in which it stood till about the year 1770, when it was purchased by Mr. Drake, as before related.

The spot whereon the battle of Bosworth field was fought, now presents little more than

than an extensive range of modern enclosures. Few traces of that memorable action which, by uniting the white rose and the red, finally terminated the unnatural contest, that for so many years had made

"—— Poor England weep in streams of blood!"

From tradition we learn, that Richard's army was encamped upon a hill, with the village of Sutton in his rear, and the wood covering his left flank; while Richmond's army was on the opposite hill, a spot well chosen for his smaller body of troops, with an extensive wood to his right, and the marsh in his front. Norfolk says,

"My lord, the enemy is past the marsh."

Near the scene of action is a Well, which still retains the name of King Richard's Well, there was formerly a flight of steps leading down to it; it is now overgrown with rushes, and running to waste. About a mile a mile diſtant, is a field called King's Field, on which Richmond is ſaid to have harrangued his ſoldiers; and near to Stoke Golding, is Crown Hill, probably the ſpot on which Henry was crowned, and below are Halloo Meadows, which probably derived the name from the ſhouts of applauſe beſtowed by his army.

We regret that the ſcenery in the vicinity of this celebrated ſpot, yields no object that is appropriate to the pencil, or that can in any degree tend to illuſtrate the page of our inſpired bard, who, in his lofty deſcription of that day, ſays,

"The king enacts more wonders than a man,
"Daring, and oppoſite to every danger."

And here, adverting to our Shakſpeare, I flatter myſelf that I may be permitted to expreſs the high gratification I felt in the courſe of this excurſion at Althorp, the ſeat of Earl Spencer, where I was honoured, by lady

lady Lucan, with a view of her elaborate and splendid illustrations of his work. They consist of portraits in miniature, of buildings, and other objects that are handed down as genuine, and illustrate or refer to some part of his compositions. These are finished with a degree of taste, correctness of design, and brilliancy of execution, far exceeding any work of genius of this kind that has ever fallen within my observation. These elegant labours do not profess to extend beyond his historical compositions, and to such only of them as relate to the history of our own country. It will, when completed, form twenty large and splendid volumes in folio, which are intended to grace the magnificent library of her son-in-law, the noble owner of this stately mansion.

Of Althorp, its superb collection of pictures, or of the superior taste displayed in its other internal decorations, it would be endless

endless to attempt to enter into a minute detail; let it suffice to say, it is the favourite residence of Earl Spencer and his accomplished Countess.

We shall now return to Welford, and resume the theme of our pursuit, the Avon, which, taking a westerly course, bends its way through a fertile and pleasant country towards Stanford, a distance of about four miles, having the villages of North and South Kilworth full in view; whose spires, occasionally breaking upon the eye, give additional beauty to the scenery. The Avon enters the grounds of Stanford Hall beneath a spacious brick bridge of one arch, and, though but a narrow stream, is yet so artfully managed, as, in its course through the park, to give the idea of a navigable river. Another bridge is thrown over it within the grounds, adjoining to which it forms a beautiful cascade; and, quitting the park, crosses the high

high road in the village, and re-assumes its narrow and humble course. Stanford Hall, the seat of the very ancient family of the Caves, stands in a low situation on the southern borders of the county of Leicester. The village of Stanford, on the opposite side of the river, is in Northamptonshire.

The house is spacious, but wants those pictorial decorations that would render it an object of attention to the traveller of taste. On the death of the late Sir Thomas Cave, about three years since, many pictures were removed to the house of the Rev. Sir Charles Cave, of Theddingworth, in Leicestershire. There is, amongst these, a curious family portrait, some account of which may perhaps prove not unacceptable to the antiquary, and probably not uninteresting to the man of gallantry, who may be gratified in knowing the colour of the garters of our virgin Queen. I am favoured by Sir Charles Cave with the following description: "The portrait is that of Sir Ambrose Cave, knt. who was high sheriff for the counties of Leicester, and Warwick, 2d Edward the sixth, 4th and 5th Philip and Mary, and 5th Elizabeth, and chancellor of the duchy of Lancaster, and one of the privy council to queen Elizabeth, in great esteem with the queen, and a most intimate friend of the great lord treasurer Burghley. Round his arm is tied a yellow garter. The circumstances which gave rise to a distinction so particular, are as follows: In the course of his attendance at court, on a ball night, the queen, while she was dancing, happened to drop her garter; which Sir Ambrose perceiving, immediately presented to her; and upon her refusing to acknowledge it, very gallantly tied it upon his left arm; declaring he would wear it for his mistress's sake as long as he lived. How long he persevered in his resolution, I know not, but this is the account I have always heard of it."

Sir Ambrose died April 2, 1568, and was buried at Stanford, where a monument is erected to his memory, which is much admired for its symmetry. In the church are likewise several other well executed monuments of the Cave family, and a considerable quantity of ancient stained glass, amongst which will be found a curious portrait of the founder of the church.

This church is decorated with a handsome organ, that formerly belonged to the banquetting room at Whitehall, which, by order of Cromwell, was taken down and sold. It was intended to be placed in the chapel of Magdalen college, Oxford, but being too small, was purchased by the Cave family for this church.

Stanford Hall, as well as the grounds about it, require some external aid, something from the hand of taste to render them more

more picturesque objects, in a situation so flat and naked, even a few groups of trees, judiciously disposed, would add to the scenery. At present, its greatest ornament is the beautiful sheet of water that is formed by our Avon, and which runs at a very proper distance from the mansion, to make the scenery more complete by the additions here suggested.

ABOUT a mile below Stanford is Swinford lordship, of which manor the heirs of the Cave family are owners. This village has nothing to attract the notice of the curious, but a tomb, erected in the church-yard, for a singular character, the Rev. Mr. Staresmore, of Catthorp, who died Jan. 1st, 1746. It was a custom with this whimsical being, at the latter end of every year, to tie a bull-dog to every apple-tree in his orchard, for the purpose of terrifying robbers. The inventory of his effects, at his death, I shall

shall present to the reader as a curiosity, from Mr. Nichols's account of him. They consist of " 30 gowns and cassocks; 53 "dogs; 100 pair of breeches; 100 pair of "boots; 400 pair of shoes; 10 wigs, and "almost always wore his own hair; 80 "waggons and carts; 80 ploughs, and used "none; 50 saddles, and furniture for the "menage; 30 wheelbarrows; walking "sticks so many, that a toyman in Lei-"cester Fields, bid his executors eight "pounds for them; 60 horses and mares; "200 pick-axes; 200 spades and shovels; "75 ladders; 240 razors. He had £700. "a year, and £1000. in money, which (he "dying intestate) fell to a ticket porter in "London. He kept one servant of each "sex whom he locked up every night. "His last employment in an evening was "to go round his premises, let loose his "dogs, and fire his gun. He lost his life "as follows: Going one morning to let out
"his

"his servants, the dogs fawned upon him
"suddenly, and threw him into a pond, where
"he was found breast high; the servants
"heard him call for assistance, but, being
"locked up, could not lend him any. His
"proverbial penury and wretchedness, drew
"upon him the contempt and ridicule of
"the inhabitants even of that humble vil-
"lage, who thought themselves disgraced
"by his meanness and avarice."

WITHOUT much diversity of scenery, the Avon winds its course through a pleasant pasture country, till it passes the small village of Lilburn. This neighbourhood is famous for the remains of an extensive Roman camp, which is as little impaired as can well be imagined, during the lapse of so many ages. The appearance of this encampment, close to the bank of our Avon, is highly beautiful; no excavation, no tree, no weed, deforms the surface; the whole of which

which is clothed with a moſt luxuriant and verdant turf. This ſplendid camp was indiſputably the Roman ſtation mentioned by Antoninus, in his Journey from London to Lincoln, under the denomination of Tripontium. The circular Tumulus, called by different writers, the Prætorium, Augurale, or Auguſtale, is ſixty-nine feet in height; having its baſe formed by a rampart, or vallum, waſhed on the north ſide by the river Avon.

This elevated ſpot, which commands a view of the whole encampment, was allotted to the General, the ſuperior officers, and young men of rank who ſerved as volunteers. On the eaſtern ſide of the prætorium, and adjoining to it, is the upper camp; the north ſide of which is, in like manner, waſhed by the river Avon. The northern vallum of the Prætorium, with that of the upper camp, form one line two hundred and

E   ſeventy

seventy-six feet in length. The inner vallum, or agger, of the upper camp, is only twenty-eight feet in height, being defended by the river. In this upper camp were the tents of the Tribunes, Prefects of the allies, and of the more honourable of the common soldiery, the Evocati, the Ablecti, and the Extraordinarii. To the south of this camp and the Prætorium, is situated the lower camp, being separated from the two former by a fosse, of which the two slopes, and the bottom, taken together, measure eighty-four feet. This space between the two camps was termed principia.

In it the tribunes administered justice; punishments were inflicted; payments were made; and the images of their gods, their altars, and the military standards were deposited. This part of a Roman encampment, seems, therefore, of all others, the

most

most likely to reward the search of the curious antiquary.

The lower camp is much larger than the upper; its southernmost outward vallum is 258 feet in length, and the height of the inner vallum or agger is 51 feet, being the side opposite to that defended by the Avon. In this camp were stationed the rank and file, under the names of Triarii, Principes, and Hastati. The whole length of the encampment measures, on the western side, 336 feet, and on the eastern, 390. Eastward adjoining the lower camp, traces of the Procestriæ are plainly discoverable. Antoninus places this camp 12 miles (plus minus) from Isaunavatia (Wedon) and nine from Vennones, (Cleybrook); and this was where the Romans placed it, and where it still remains; although Camden has removed it to Towcester, Horsley, to Buckby, and Dr. Henry to Rugby. Dr. Horsley, in his map of Britain, gives the Roman public roads and omits the names of the lesser towns situate by the sides of the roads; he therefore sets down Bugby, instead of the village of Buckby (which is between Daventry and Northampton) and Dr. Henry, consulting all the maps of England he could meet with, could not find any such town as Buckby, whose situation and name so nearly corresponded with that of Bugby, as Rugby; and therefore thought he had happily corrected an erratum in Horsley's map by substituting Rugby for Bugby. The identity of the spot receives further confirmation from the circumstance of Antoninus's having omitted the mention of it in his journies from York, through Lincoln, to London; and from Vallum (the rampart of Severus between England and Scotland) ad Portum Ritupis (Sandwich) because, had the Tripontium, like the other stations, been situated *immediately upon* the military way, it would like them

them of neceffity have been paffed *through* by Antoninus, and confequently fet down in his lift; but, lying at fome little diftance, being rather more than half a mile out of his road, it was *paffed by*, and therefore omitted. Thus the fituation contributes to juftify the omiffion, and the omiffion affifts in verifying the fituation.

This correct defcription of the encampment will I flatter myfelf be a means of removing thofe doubts and differences of opinion, that have exifted among the learned for ages paft.

About a mile diftant from Tripontium, on the right, ftands Coton Houfe, a fpacious manfion of ftone erected by Abraham Grimes, Efq. It is fituated on an eminence and commands an extenfive profpect over a part of Northamptonfhire, including the confpicuous range of hills, extending from

Da-

Daventry to Warwickshire. Near the site of this house, formerly stood an ancient edifice, the property of Sir William Dixwell, Bart. ancestor to its present possessor.

About five miles distant from this spot is Ledger's Ashby, the seat of —— Ashley, Esq. and formerly that of Robert Catesby, Esq. the principal actor in that celebrated conspiracy formed in the 2d year of James I. in 1604, and known by the name of the Gunpowder-Treason plot.

This venerable mansion is in a perfect habitable state, although it seems to have received little addition, or alteration within the last two hundred years. It does not appear by any historical or traditional account, that at any time Catesby received the conspirators within this mansion, but from the general understanding of the neighbourhood, they met in a large apartment over the gate
at

at the entrance to the houfe. Here Catefby frequently held interviews with Piercy a defcendant of the Northumberland family, and who appears to have been the firft perfon to whom he imparted his intention. The infide of the room of which the following is a fketch, is fpacious, and fitted up fuitable to the tafte of thofe times.

It is lined with old oak pannels, and has a large gothic bow window at one end of it, in which remain two or three pieces of ancient ftained glafs. A large ftone chimney

ney piece is likewife ftanding that accords with the ftyle of building at or a fhort time before that period, and remains like the reft of the chamber with no apparent alteration fince the beginning of the laft century.

A SKETCH of the outfide of this room and the gateway beneath it, I have likewife confidered as not unworthy a place in this work.

Not having seen prints of either of these objects before, the novelty of them may with some readers plead an apology for their introduction; but to the antiquary it is presumed they will require none.

Catesby appears to have been a man of great respectability and property in his county, and of no mean talents. He certainly stood so high in the minds of the parties to whom he communicated his horrid designs, that they with a full confidence embraced, and became participators in his direful projects. In the spring, and summer of 1604, this plot appears to have been first divulged by Catesby, and in all probability in this very apartment. About that period, we learn from Hume's History of England, that " they hired a house in Piercy's name, ad" joining to that in which the Parliament " was to assemble, and that towards the end " of that year they began their opera" tions." For the nature and discovery of this extraordinary plot, which is marked with a degree of bigotry to religious tenets, from whatever source derived, that is without a parallel in the annals of mankind, I refer the reader to the elegant and sagacious author beforementioned.

WITHIN the parish of Ashby-Ledgers, stands Ashby-lodge, the property of George Arnold, Esq.—The house, which was an old family seat, has received very considerable additions and improvements. The inducement however for introducing it in this place, is not only its having been made the repository of a valuable collection of pictures, but the taste which has been displayed in improving the face of the country, together with a magnificent lake which is equalled by few in this island.

PASSING this lake by a pleasant and well imagined road, we are led to admire a richly varied and extensive scenery, comprising a

fertile

fertile and verdant champaign country, terminated by a range of hills, that gradually recede from the eye, and melt in the ethereal diftance:—and the rocky fcenery, immediately through which the road is formed, powerfully arrefts our attention by its wild and rugged parts, which conftitute a noble fore-ground to the furrounding landfcape.

RETURNING to our Avon, we fhall accompany its banks to the village of Catthorpe, about a mile below Lillburn, a village although with little but its retired fituation to render it worthy of attention, cannot yet be left unnoticed in thefe hiftorical remarks on our gentle river. Indeed, after having fuffered a fingle page of this volume to be occupied by the memorials of fuch a wretch as Starefmore, I could as little juftify it to myfelf, as to the public, were I here to pafs over in filence the elegant

and

and accomplished John Dyer. He was born in 1700, received his education at Westminster School, under Dr. Friend, and was intended by his father to be bred up in the pursuit of his own profession that of the law: but a predilection for the fine arts led him from those phlegmatic and severer studies, to the more attracting ones of drawing and painting, in the which he is said to have made considerable progress as a pupil under Jonathan Richardson, and during his travels in this country; though he attained still greater perfection in the course of his excursions through Italy. Of his works however as an artist we know but little, he appears to have quitted that profession for one more congenial to his feelings. He was delicate in his frame of body, and was by the narrowness of his fortune and the difficulties he encountered in the support of a numerous family compelled to go into orders; and, during some part of the time in which

Staresmore vegetated in this place, discharged there the duties of his new profession, having accepted the scanty provision of the rectory of this small and obscure parish. Under the pressure of the same difficulties, he was afterwards unhappily induced by an ampler benefice to remove into Lincolnshire; when his feeble constitution soon yielded to the moist atmosphere and damps of that country. By his poem on the ruins of Rome, to those who are conversant with the higher species of poetry, the sublimity of his genius is well known; while by the softer beauties of his Gronger-hill, the elegance of his mind has become familiar to all, who, with any knowledge of the English language, have the least relish for poetry. In this work the Connoisseur will acknowledge, that he can trace the original bent and direction of his mind; and that it carries with it the most pregnant evidence of its being the production of a painter, as well

well as that of a poet. I do not hesitate to lay before my readers the following poetical epistle of his to a friend in town, as it is not to be met with in the common editions of his works, and as it exhibits at once a faithful portraiture of the gentle virtues of its amiable author, and a very striking specimen of that imitative harmony, with which his works abound more than of any of our poets.

   Have my friends in the town, in the busy, gay, town,
      Forgot such a man as John Dyer?
   Or heedless despise they, or pity the Clown,
      Whose bosom no pageantries fire?

   No matter, no matter—Content in the shades—
      (Contented? Why every thing charms me)
   " Fall in tunes all adown the green steep, ye Cascades,"
      Till hence rigid virtue alarms me.

   Till outrage arise, or till misery needs
      The swift, the intrepid avenger;
   Till sacred Religion or Liberty bleeds:—
      Then mine be the deed and the danger.

                                Alas!

Alas! what a folly, that wealth and domain
  We keep up in ſin and in ſorrow!
Immenſe is the toil, yet the labour how vain!
  Is not life to be over to-morrow?·

Then glide on my moments, the few that I have,
  Smooth, ſhaded and quiet, and even;
While gently my body deſcends to the grave,
  And my Spirit ariſes to Heaven!

SEC-

SECTION III.

A LITTLE below Catthorp, we reach Dow-bridge, formerly the Tripontium of the Romans. This bridge was built about twenty years since by order of the Commissioners of the Turnpike-road leading from Lutterworth to Banbury. It consists of five arches, which are formed of brick and stone Coignes. The scene, though simple, aided by a group of cattle then passing, had sufficient attraction, in the meridian of a summer sun, to induce us to attempt a sketch of it, as a picturesque view.

A LARGE stone, taken from the old bridge, is preserved and placed on the centre arch, on the sides in letters almost obliterated, appear the words, Warwick-shire,

shire, Leicestershire, and Northamptontonshire; this being the point where these three counties unite. In the place where this bridge is erected, there stood two small ones, the larger was designed for carriages; the lesser, which was evidently Roman, probably for horse and foot passengers, as it had only a very low parapet, not exceeding six inches in height. These bridges were not passable in times of flood, which, from the smallness of the bed of the river and the level of the valley, are here very frequent. Hence, it is not unreasonable to conjecture, that when the Romans had a station here, they must have had a third bridge, for the purpose of securing to themselves a ready communication with the adjoining country and encampment. And this idea seems to be strongly supported by the name of Tripontium, given to their encampment at Lillburn, of which we treated in the last Section.

ABOUT

About one mile below this bridge, the village of Clifton appears, on the South of the Avon, on a small eminence: this place derives its name from its situation, Clive signifying, in the Saxon language, not only a rocky place, but any shelving ground. On the opposite bank, about the same distance, stands the hamlet of Newt n, on the borders of Leicestershire; a modern brick bridge of one arch is here thrown across the Avon, which takes its name from this hamlet. A little below the bridge is an aquæduct that conveys the water of the Oxford canal across the river Avon, and the valley through which it passes. At the vilage of Brownsover, our Avon is joined by the river Swift, which rises near Knaptoft, in Leicestershire, and taking Lutterworth in its course, enters Warwickshire at Bensford bridge, over which was carried the Roman road, called the Watling-street. The Swift cannot be passed over without adverting to the remarkable circumstance of its having received the ashes of the famous reformer John Wickliff, who died Rector of Lutterworth, in 1384. He was struck with a paralysis while preaching at his parish church, and as his parishioners were conveying him from thence in a chair to his Rectory-house, expired in his way thither.

The chair yet exists, it is made of oak,

and

and, for the gratification of the curious, a sketch of it is here annexed.

The body of the pulpit likewife remains,

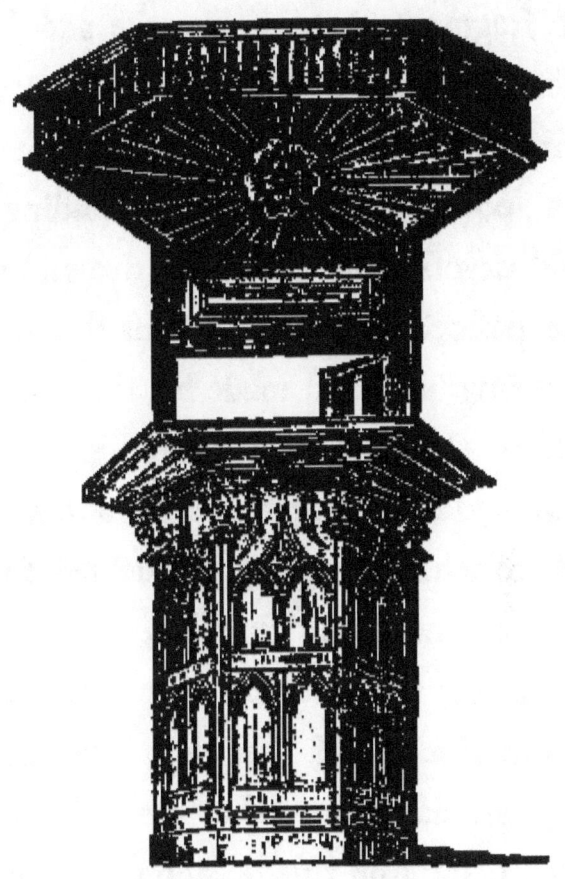

but the founding-board which had been beaten down many years ago, when the roof of the church fell in, was removed into,

into an obscure part of that edifice, and, although but little damaged, has been suffered to lie unnoticed, and a new one has been injudiciously erected in its stead. Of that fragment, I have likewise added a representation, in which I have aimed at restoring it to the situation, in which it stood as a powerful instrument in aiding the fervid devotion of this primitive and venerable pastor. I cannot dismiss this subject, interesting as it is made by the relation it bears to the lives and sufferings of those undaunted and disinterested servants of their God, to whom posterity is indebted for the purity of the Christian faith, without adverting to the peculiar rancour of the Romish Zealots of that day, who proverbially vindictive as they may have been thought, seem on this occasion to have been inflamed with a more than ordinary and antichristian spirit, and, to have carried their resentments beyond the grave. For in 1415,

1415, thirty-one years after he had lain quietly interred, they dug up his body, burnt the bones, and threw the afhes into the river, at the bridge, in the lower part of the town. This acrimonious zeal of their leader, Dr. Fox, then Bifhop of Lincoln, appears to have far exceeded the orders of the pious fathers his employers, in the council of Conftance, who only envying his repofe in confecrated ground, directed no more than that his remains

" Procul ab ecclefiæ fepulturâ jactari."

On the fouth fide of the Avon, nearly oppofite to the village of Brownfover, is the town of Rugby, which ftands on an eafy afcent about half a mile from the river. This town is written in Domefday-book, Rocheberie, and in later times Rokeby. In the Dictionnaire Celtique, the name is faid to be of Celtic origin, and derived from Ruc a river, a river, and Bye a town, which agrees with its fituation.

DUGDALE fays, "here was a little caftle at Rokeby, which ftood about a furlong from the church northwards; as it is to be feen by the banks of earth, and part of the moat yet remaining." He is of opinion, that it was built in the time of King Stephen, and demolifhed by command of King Henry II. The fite, whereon the caftle ftood, is ftrongly marked by the form and elevation of the earth and the foffe yet remaining that furround it.

THESE veftiges of antiquity terminate the enclofures adjoining the houfe of the Rev. Dr. Clare, by whofe attention they are preferved in fuch a verdant and cultivated ftate, as to render them no fmall addition to his profpect. The tower of the church is faid to have been built with part of of the stone taken from the ruin of the castle; it is the largest structure I remember to have seen, that stands without buttresses. A principal support to this town is its freeschool, which was founded in the ninth year of Elizabeth, by Lawrence Sheriff, a grocer of London; who also endowed four alms-houses in this place. The present head master, Dr. James, by his great assiduity, temper, and learning, happily supports this noble institution; and which has been raised by his character and unremitting labours to the consequence and estimation, which it at present holds—and here although contrary to the opinion of Dr. Henry, that no Roman ways or relics are in this place to be found, yet may Rugby boast of superior excellencies,—the language of that nation in all its Augustan purity. The extensive liberality of the founder, may possibly create a wish in the reader to know something of his history: He was a native of Brown's-over, the village we have juft paffed on the bank of our Avon. He was of very low origin, but, making his way to London, by application and frugality in his bufinefs of a grocer, became one of the wealthieft citizens of his day. His confequence at that time cannot be more fully fhewn, than by a curious paffage in Fox's Book of Martyrs; which although of fome length, yet as it in a ftrong degree exhibits the rancorous quality and character of the times and wretched policy of our rulers, may not be unacceptable to our readers at the prefent hour, in which the conduct of ftate affairs is regulated by principles of much greater liberality.

" Soon after the ftir of Wiat, and the
" troubles that happened to Queen Mary for
" that caufe, it fortuned one Robert Farrer, a
" haberdafher of London, dwelling near un-
" to Newgate-market, in a certain morning
" to

" to be at the Rose Tavern (from whence
" he was seldom absent), and falling to his
" common drink, as he was ever accustom-
" ed, and having in his company three other
" companions like to himself, it chanced the
" same time one Lawrence Sheriff, grocer,
" dwelling also not far from thence, to come
" into the said tavern, and finding there the
" said Farrer, (to whom of long time he
" had borne good will) sate down in the
" seat to drink with him, and Farrer having
" in his full cups, and not having consider-
" ation who were present, began to talk at
" large, and namely against the lady *Eliza-*
" *beth*, and said that *Jill* hath bin one of
" the chief doers of this rebellion of *Wiatt*,
" and before all be done, she and all the
" hereticks her partakers, shall well under-
" stand of it. Some of them hope that
" she shall have the crown, but she and
" they (I trust) that so hope, shall hop
" headless, or be fried with faggots before
" she come to it. The aforesaid Lawrence
" Sheriff,

"Sheriff, grocer, being then servant unto
"the lady Elizabeth, and sworn unto her
"Grace, could no longer forbear his old
"acquaintance, and neighbour *Farrer* in
"speaking so unreverantly of his mistress,
"but said unto him: Farrer I have loved
"thee as a neighbour, and have had a good
"opinion of thee, but hearing of thee that
"I now hear, I defie thee, and tell thee I
"am her Graces sworn servant, and she is
"a princess, and the daughter of a noble
"King, and it evil becometh thee to call
"her a *Jill*, and for thy so saying, I say
"thou art a Knave, and I will complain
"upon thee. Do thy worst said Farrer:
"for that I said, I will say again, and so
"Sheriff came from his company.

"Shortly after, the said Sheriff, tak-
"ing an honest neighbour with him, went
"before the commissioners to complain;
"the which commissioners sate then at Bon-
"ner's the bishop of London's house, beside
"Paul's,

" Paul's, and there were present, Bonner
" then being the chief commissioner, the
" Lord Mordaunt, Sir John Baker, Dr. Dar-
" byshire, Chancellor to the Bishop, Dr.
" Story, Dr. Harpsfield, and others.

" THE aforesaid Sheriff coming before
" them, declared the manner of the said
" Robert Farrer's talk against the lady Eli-
" zabeth, Bonner answered, peradventure
" you took him worse than he meant.

" YEA my Lord said Dr. Story, if you
" knew the man as I do, you would say
" there is not a better Catholick, nor an
" honester man in the city of London.

" WELL said Sheriff, my Lord, she is
" my gracious lady and mistress, and is not
" to be suffered that such a varlet as he is
" should call so honourable a princess by
" the name of a *Jill* : and I saw yesterday
" in the court, that my Lord Cardinal Pool,
" meet-

" meeting her in the chamber of presence,
" kneeled down on his knees and kissed her
" hand; and I saw also, that King Philip
" meeting her, made her much obeysance,
" and that his knee touched the ground;
" and then, me thinketh, it were too much
" to suffer such a varlet as this is to call her
" a *Jill*, and to wish them to hop headless
" that shall wish her Grace to enjoy the pos-
" session of the crown, when God shall send
" it unto her, as in the right of her inherit-
" ance. Yea? stay there, quoth Bonner,
" when God sendeth it unto her, let her en-
" joy it. But truly (said he) the man that
" spake the words that you have reported,
" meant nothing against the lady Elizabeth
" your mistress, and no more do we: but
" he, like an honest and zealous man, feared
" the alteration of Religion, which every
" good man ought to fear: and therefore
" (said Bonner) good man go your ways
" home, and report well of us toward your
" mistress, and we will send for Farrer and
                                    " rebuke

" rebuke him for his rash and undiscrete
" words, and, we trust, he will not do
" the like again: and thus Sheriff came
" away, and Farrer had a flap with a Fox
" tail."

I CANNOT quit the neighbourhood of Rugby, without communicating some information I here received, on the subject of water freezing first at the bottom of rivers. I am induced to offer this in support of a remark I formerly made on the same subject, with respect to the river Thames (vol 1. p. 35.) in the vicinity of Lechlade, in Gloucestershire. This part of our river is not navigable: the course of it is interrupted by a number of mills, and the millers have consequently the best means of becoming acquainted with this phenomenon, and the more so, as these frosts seldom happen there more than once during a winter; and though I have met with an opinion to this effect generally circulating in this

neigh-

neighbourhood, I yet altogether found my account of this singular process of nature in her works, upon the authority of a person, who has occupied the mill near Rugby for almost forty years. He says that the icy particles do not in every frost arise from the bottom of the river, but only in one particular kind of frost, which the miller denominates, the *Anchor-Frost*. The freezing commences at the bottom of the floodgates, which he first becomes sensible of by the passage of the water being stopped at that point, and is plainly perceived at the flood-gates in its progress from the bottom to the top, to fill up and successively close the cracks that appear in the surface. They attempt to draw the sluices, but in vain: and with no better success endeavor with long poles to break the ice; these poles when drawn out of the river, are incrusted with light, hollow, and honeycombed ice: After these frosts the river always overflows its banks. Other masses of ice in various parts,

parts, rise to the surface, and are brought down by the stream. The upper part of the water is not frozen, and by the time the sun has been four hours above the horizon, the whole is dissolved, and the mill no longer impeded in its operation. It may not be improper to add, that the same kind of frost has been observed in America, and is called by the same peculiar name, (viz.) *Anchor Frost*.

THE accuracy of the above relation, as well as the popular opinion of a similar report in other places, I cannot be mistaken in, but its causes and principles I must leave to the discussion of those, who are better skilled in the great study of natural philosophy.

SECTION IV.

QUITTING Rugby we pass a handsome modern bridge of three circular arches constructed of stone, thrown across the Avon at about half a mile distant from the town. The river from hence winds gently through a fertile and expanded valley, till we reach the village of Newbold; which from its eminent situation commands a beautiful and extensive prospect on every side. The canal, that appears in the annexed view, is conducted through a subterraneous passage beneath part of the church-yard of Newbold, and from this point highly encreases the beauty of the surrounding scene, which includes an extended view of the meandering course of our gentle Avon through a verdant space of fertile valleys. The spire of the church in the distance of the landscape belongs to the village of Bilton, which may well be considered as classical ground, having been the residence of Mr. Addison, a name that will ever be held in esteem by the admirer of sound criticism, chaste humour, and a correct and attic style of composition. Veneration for the character of this eminent man leads me to view the situation of his retreat, which stands about a mile distant from the bank of the Avon.

The preceding view is a faithful representation

prefentation of the exterior of this houfe, which though it cannot be truly denominated picturefque, may yet have a claim to attention, as it remains precifely in the ftate it was at the deceafe of its former poffeffor; nor has the interior fuffered much change in its form, or decoration. The furniture and pictures hold their places with an apparent facred attention to his memory: among the latter, are three of himfelf, at different periods of his life, in each of which is ftrongly marked with the pencil, the eafe of the gentleman, and open and ingenuous character of the friend to humanity. Two good portraits are likewife hanging, near his own, of his friend Mr. Secretary Craggs. Some others, of Van Dyck, Van Somers, Lilly, &c. that were purchafed by Mr. Addifon, are to be found in other apartments fufficient to evince that his tafte was not confined to writing alone. In the grounds a long walk of beautiful
Spanifh

Spanish chesnuts and oaks running in a strait line, still hold their primitive appearance; here he was accustomed to pass the hours in that musing, and in those reflections, from which the public have gathered so rich a fruit, it retains the name of Addison's walk: This form of a strait line, is that to which in his earliest youth, he seems to have been attached, as part of the walks in Magdalen College, which are fashioned upon this model, still pass there under his name.

The Spanish oaks in these grounds are said to have been the first that were planted in this country; the acorns were given to him by his friend Craggs, who brought them from Spain.

In a kind of hermitage in this walk, I found the following verses,

" Se-

"Sequestered from the world, oh! let me dwell,
"With contemplation in this lonely cell
"By mortal eye unseen, I will explore
"The various works of Nature's bounteous store,
"Revisit oft each flower whose blossom fair
"With fragrant sweets perfumes the ambient air
"Pry into every shrub, and mark its way
"From birth to growth, from growth to sure decay:
"Or else with humble thoughts my eyes I'll bend,
"And view the near resemblance of my end
"Then think of death, and of eternal days
"Learn how to die, my Maker how to praise:
"All ways despise, that draw my mind from this,
"Then strive to gain an endless age of bliss."

I do not know that these lines were Mr. Addison's, but there is something in their moral turn, as well as their versification, that renders them not unworthy a recital. This estate was purchased by Mr. Addison in the year 1711, of the younger son of Sir William Boughton, for the sum of ten thousand pounds; in the purchase he was assisted by his brother Mr. Gulstone Addison, Governor of Fort St. George, at Madrass, in which

which station he succeeded Governor Pitt, distinguished by the appellation of Diamond Pitt.

At the decease of Mr. Addison in 1719, this estate came to his widow the Countess of Warwick, from whom it devolved on their daughter, the present Mrs. Addison, whom I had the honour of seeing, at this visit, with no small degree of respect and veneration. This lady was born about a twelvemonth before the death of her father, who as some vague reports in the country say, left a large trunk of manuscripts, with a strict injunction that they should not be opened till her decease; if this be true, the polite and learned, may at a future day expect what may yet further magnify the revered name of Addison.

To the westward of Bilton, the Avon directs its course towards Little Lawford, which

which stands in the parish of Newbold upon Avon.

APPROACHING the grounds where Lawford-hall, the seat of the Boughton's, formerly stood, we pass the spot on which Dugdale says " there was antiently a capital " messuage, and divers cottages, belonging to " the monks of Pipewell Abbey." Nothing remains of these buildings at present, but a large corn-mill on the bank of the river which is directly opposite to the site of ground on which Lawford-hall stood till within these five years, when it was taken down by the late Sir Edward Boughton, Bart. from whom the manor and site was purchased by John Caldecot, Esq. of Rugby, its present possessor. No part is standing of this ancient seat but its stabling, which is now applied to the purposes of a farm-house.

K FOR

For the gratification of the curious, the annexed sketch of Lawford-hall is here given, as it appeared a short time before it was taken down.

The fate of the late Sir Theodosius Boughton, by the horrid machinations of Captain Donellan, who married his sister, are too recent in the memory of every one to need a repetition.

In Lawford-hall, I am told, a room was preserved as the bed-chamber of an ancestor

tor of the family, who, in the time of Elizabeth having lost an arm, went afterwards by the appellation of one-handed Boughton. After his death, the room was reported to be haunted, and as such, many attempts were made to sleep in it, but in vain; and such is the credulity of the lower people, that it was with difficulty any labourer could be prevailed on to assist in pulling it down: the ghost of this one-handed gentleman I was told, by persons on the spot, had been frequently seen by their fathers, riding across the neighbouring grounds in a coach and six, and with the same air of confidence, I was informed, that within the present century, his perturbed spirit had been laid by a numerous body of the clergy, who conjured it into a phial, and threw it into a marle pit opposite the house. Nor does the family seem to have been exempt from a similar superstition and belief in ghosts, for it is told of the late Sir Theodosius's

dofius's father, that, being visited by his neighbour, the late Sir Francis Skipwith, and walking together near the marle pit, Sir Francis observed that he thought there must be many fish in that pond, and that he should be glad to try it; to which Sir Theodosius gravely replied; no, that I cannot consent to, for the spirit of my ancestor, the one handed Boughton, lies there.

ABOUT half a mile below this spot, on the bank of the Avon, stands the once celebrated Newnham Bath; famed for the cure of scorbutic and other disorders. It is said to have had great efficacy in closing and healing green wounds. The water is considered as a weak chalybeate. It has a milky taste, and issues from a mineral spring about a mile distant, from whence, passing a lime pit, it receives its chief salubrious quality. This well is still much frequented, and would probably be much more so, were the roads kept in in a passable state. The country around it is beautiful, and capable of infinite improvement. On the south-side of the river, as we approach Newnham Regis, the village of Church Lawford, on an easy eminence, forms a very picturesque object. The manor, on the attainder of the Duke of Buckingham in the 13th of Henry the Eighth, came to the crown, and was afterwards granted, by licence of Queen Elizabeth, to Thomas Leigh, Alderman of London, of whom we shall have occasion to say more in the course of this undertaking. The lordship is the property of the Duke of Buccleugh in right of his dutchess. He is likewise proprietor of the ancient village of Newnham Regis. About a mile below this place, at a small distance from the bank of the Avon, the town as its name imparts, appears by legal proceedings in the thirteenth of Edward the First to have been in the possession of the King. The body of the venerable chapel of this

this place is now by order of its proprietor taking down, but the tower, I am informed, is to remain: the chapel has been long in difuse. In pulling down this edifice, the pavement giving way, not far from the furface a perfect fkeleton, fuppofed to have been that of the founder, was difcovered, and not far from it a feal. The altar of this church was decorated with fome good paintings in frefco, well preferved, which feem to bear the character and ftyle of painting of the time of James I. the defigns are made from fubjects in the New Teftament, and in their manner are not unlike thofe of Reubens, but have more the air of the Italian fchool. I have preferved a fragment of this work as a fpecimen. The fame love of the arts that induced me carefully to preferve this fragment, impels me to deviate a little from the courfe of the river to the feat of the ancient family of the Fieldings, Earls of Denbigh, at Newnham Padox, fo called from the fmall park adjoining;

adjoining; and to diftinguifh it from the Newnham we have juft quitted. The prefent noble earl has felected, with much tafte, fome exceeding good pictures of the old mafters, which added to the collection of family portraits by Van Dyck, pictures by Rembrandt, and other eminent artifts, render this manfion well worthy the notice of the connoiffeur.

Amongst other reliques of antiquity, I was fhewn by his lordfhip the dagger with which Felton ftabbed the Duke of Buckingham: of this dagger I have annexed a fketch,

and with it the account given me by his lordfhip,

ship, which is as follows:—This dagger was brought from Southwich, the house of Sir Daniel Norton, within five miles of Portsmouth, where the court then, in 1628, was held, and at which place the murder was committed. The person, who brought it, was one Firebrace, valet de chambre to the Duke, and who was the ancestor of the late Sir Cordel Firebrace, Baronet: it was brought to the Lady Susannah Villers, sister to the duke, who was then married to Sir William Fielding, afterwards the first Earl of Denbigh, and ancestor to the present earl. The length of the dagger is eight inches, the blades near four and a half, the breadth of it near the handle, which is of ivory, one inch and a half: the inner sides of the blades and handle, are flat, and move on two small pivots, which give firmness to the gripe when the blades are opened. There can be no doubt but that this traditional account has been handed down from generation to generation,

ration, in this very antient and illustrious family, but as the instrument with which this bloody act was perpetrated, is very differently described by so very respectable authors as Lord Clarendon, Sir Simon D'Ewes, and Dr. Wotton (none of whom appear to have had any communication with each other, and one of whom asserts that it was bought of a cutler, on Tower-hill, for ten-pence) from this contradictory testimony the public must be left to draw their own conclusions.

From Newnham Regis the river Avon, with little diversity of scenery, runs nearly in a strait direction, till we reach Bretford bridge, a distance of about two miles. This antient stone structure is in the Gothic style, and consists of five arches. The bridge, though a conspicuous object on our river, is yet unaccompanied by any such feature in landscape as can give it a claim to the appellation of picturesque or beautiful. In this place there was formerly a small cell for nuns, founded by the son of Geffery Clinton, who erected the Castle and Priory of Kenilworth, but the first votress not liking the situation, she passed away the lands to the canons of the last mentioned place.

SEC-

SECTION V.

COMBE Abbey, the venerable residence of Lord Craven, is about two miles north of the Avon from Bretford Bridge. So stately a pile of building, though not immediately on the bank of the river, may yet be considered as one of its great ornaments.

The small scale on which the annexed view is made, though it does not admit of a very minute or detailed representation, will yet, from its fidelity, give a general idea of the place.

This Abbey was founded in the reign of King Stephen, by Richard de Camvill, a man of great piety, and a warm friend to the Cistercian monks, a religious order then newly transplanted into England. For the maintenance

tenance of this inftitution, the founder gave unto Gilbert, abbot of the monaftery of our bleffed Lady of Waverly, in Surry, his lordfhip of Smite, which he and his heirs held of the King, by the fervice of a knight's fee. The abbey derives its name of Combe, or Cumbe, from the Saxon, and in that language fignified a hollow, or a valley: Cwmm likewife, in the Britifh, implies Vallis, or Convallis; and the word Cumbe is to this day ufed as a provincial name, in the north of England, for a hollow veffel of wood in which it is ufual to fteep barley, or malt.

From Dugdale it appears, that the monaftery of Waverly, in Surry, was the firft inftitution of this order in our country; and in fupport of this idea, he introduces the following quaint lines of our old poet, Robert of Gloucefter:

" Houfes of religion, as I feide or I wene,
" Kynge Henry lovede moche as hit was wel fene,
" For

" For the ordre of Gray Monkes thorwg then men brougt
" Furft here into Englonde, and peraventer men him bifougt
" As in the abby of Waverle that hit furft become,
" As in the eigte and twenty yeer of his Kyngdome."

THIS order was originally eftablifhed under the aufpices of the Duke of Burgundy, in 1098, at a place called Ciftieux, from whence it derives its name.

IT may not be thought uninterefting, perhaps, if we advert to the hiftory and ufages of this auftere clafs of monks, who, by the rules of their order, were not permitted to wear either leather, linen, or fine woollen cloth; nor, except on a journey, to put on breeches, and thefe, on their return, they were compelled to deliver up cleanly wafhed. Thus we find that the Sans Culottes of a neighbouring country are not the firft of that order; and though their armies under that denomination have increafed fo wonder-
fully

fully in number, as to aſtoniſh all Europe, yet it appears that the ſans-culotted Ciſtercians multiplied in a proportion nearly ſimilar: for this order, which with us originally conſiſted of only twenty-one monks, did, within fifty-five years, increaſe ſo rapidly as to produce ſcarcely leſs than five hundred abbies, and, no doubt, according to the habit of the order, in equal ratio "Monks, and "friars, white, black, or grey, with all their "trumpery." The alarming acceſſion to this increaſe of church militants, occaſioned a general chapter of the abbots and biſhops to be convened, in which it was ordained, that no further endowments of that order ſhould be permitted.

Some part of the original Ciſtercian foundation of Combe Abbey may be ſtill remaining; but, venerable as the older parts of the building appear, they are yet, I preſume, of a more modern date. This edifice has

has of late years been preserved with the utmost care and attention; and the principal front and cloysters, by the taste and judgment of the architect in conducting the repairs, still retain their ancient and Gothic style.

The internal part of the cloysters, indeed, have undergone some very material changes from their original destination; for, instead of crucifixes, holy water, and saints bowing under their own, or the iniquities of their worshippers, we now find their places supplied by the horns of animals of every denomination, from the days of Nimrod to the present.—Within this venerable building are many noble and spacious apartments, decorated with pictures of so superior a class as to render them worthy the attention of the connoisseur; while others, of a more curious kind, will be found not less attractive to the antiquary.

The

The western front of this building is from a design of Inigo Jones, and is not unworthy his name. From the apartments in this aspect, the views are beautiful; and in one of them, which includes the antient city of Coventry, the elegant spire of its principal church forms a very striking feature: the easy winding of a spacious sheet of water, upwards of two miles in length, that runs at a proper distance from the front of the abbey, highly enriches the scenery of the very extensive park in which this antient mansion stands. Returning towards the Avon, we pass the village of Brinklow, where formerly stood an antient castle belonging to the Mowbrays, of which there are scarcely any vestiges. The famous John Rous, the antiquary mentioned in a former section, was descended from an antient family of that name, who were natives of this town. The remains of a Roman encampment at Brinklow, are yet existing, and in a more perfect state

state than might be supposed from the lapse of so many ages: they stand upon the Roman fosse way; and the eminent situation of the Prætorium commands a very beautiful view of Warwick, Coventry, and the surrounding country. This encampment is about one mile above Bretford Bridge; from which place the river, in an easy and narrow channel, pursues its course towards Wolston, a distance of about two miles. The scenery on the approach to this place is peculiarly attractive: in the fore ground is an antient stone bridge, with a gentle fall of water issuing through one of its arches; while the venerable tower of the church, rising in a due distance, is happily relieved by the diversified scenery in the grounds of Gen. Scott, through which the gentle Avon winds its easy and serpentine course.

OPPOSITE to Wolston, on the southern bank

bank of the river, is another remain of a Roman encampment, many parts of which still appear in great perfection. Here was antiently a castle, of which there are now but few fragments. In the reign of Henry I. it is recorded that military service was performed here, and that it was denominated Brandon, or Brandune castle. We find, in the reign of Henry III. a special grant to Nicholas de Verdon, empowering him to erect a gallows at Bretford, being one, as it should seem, in the number of royal privileges appertaining to his castle of Brandon. Delegations of authority, in these times happily beyond, and ought never to have been annexed to military command.

About a mile below Wolston is Brandon mill, employed in making a coarse brown paper for the use of hot-pressers: it stands on a branch of the Avon, about a quarter of a mile

mile from the main stream. Ricton church, a small distance from the Avon, is situated on an eminence, and commands a very extensive and diversified prospect. A bridge is built across the river in this vicinity, and takes its name from the village, over which the high road leads from London to Coventry: from the latter place it is distant about six miles.

Two miles and a half from hence, we pass the pleasant village of Bubnell, or, as it was antiently written, Bubenhalle. Below this place is a handsome stone bridge, which bears the name of Broken Bridge; but its perfect state of repair would rather lead to a conjecture that its proper appellation should have been Brooks Bridge. The Avon from hence enters Stonely park, where a handsome stone bridge of four arches, thrown across it, is called Cloud Bridge, and separates Bubnell from the village of Starton. The name of this bridge is from Clude, which, in the Saxon language, signifies a rocky situation. In this neighbourhood there was antiently a hermitage, and a chapel, at which, says Dugdale, Edmund the hermit served, for whose maintenance certain parcels of land lying in Starton, were given by William, surnamed Hasteler, brother to one Simon, cook to King Henry I. Edmund was buried in the chapel here, but his shrine was not able to protect it from being burnt and pillaged by thieves. After this sacrilege, the honest prior of Kenelworth entered upon the lands, and appropriated the whole of them to the use of that monastery. Thus the ruin which was effected by one set of Marauders, was fully accomplished by one of those who, though not in professed habits of rapine and plunder, have too often been found little better than wolves in sheeps' cloathing.—This same worthy prior, we find, was presented by the hundred, in the twenty-sixth

sixth year of Edward III. for not keeping the antient bridge of Clude in repair, as his predecessors had done time out of mind; but the goodly priest, having proved that " no " certain person was obliged to repair it, in " regard it had been built by the hermit as " abovesaid, and moreover that there being " another bridge near at hand, there was no " necessity to keep up this, he was ac-" quitted."

IN the midst of Stonely park, about a mile from Cloud bridge, is another stone structure, built across the Avon, consisting of three arches, erected in 1674. Not far from hence our stream receives the aid of the river Sow, which rises in Staffordshire, and passing the neighbouring village of Stonely, beneath a spacious bridge, enters these beautiful grounds, where, by art, it is spread into a considerable breadth of water. Stonely derives its name from the quality of the soil

on

on which it stands, which is of a rocky nature. In this neighbourhood William the Conqueror had feeding for two thousand hogs. The singular customs appertaining to this manor, are specified by Dugdale, to whom I refer the curious reader. The additional breadth which this stream, by its skilful management, has obtained, gives it, at its first approach to the abbey, the appearance of a spacious navigable river.

Stonely abbey was founded in 1154, the first year of Henry the Second, as a monastery for monks of the Cistercian order. Three sides of the quadrangle of this venerable abbey are yet standing; the fourth was taken down on erecting the present mansion, which was built from the design of Mr. Smith, of Warwick, in the beginning of the present century. The Grand Façade is a regular and handsome piece of architecture, of the Corinthian order; but it has, by some strange

strange fatality that I am sorry to say attends many of our capital buildings, been totally misplaced. It stands not where the grand front should be, but as a side front, or rather the gavel end, by which means the river passes some of the out offices, and inferior parts of the mansion. The apartments within the new building are spacious, and those of the antient abbey that remain are used as bed chambers and out offices. The groien'd arches beneath the abbey are in perfect repair, and make as excellent wine cellars now, as they ever did in the time of the good fathers, their former possessors; of whose charity, whatever may have been said, we are happy in according with the general voice, that they are every way exceeded by the munificent lady its present owner; who, without the austerities or obligations of a religious order, fulfils all its duties, and more than equals all its virtues.

THE

The only part of the antient building, that appears in the annexed view, is the gate houſe, which, Dugdale ſays, was built by the ſixteenth abbot, who died in 1349. On the front there is yet remaining a large eſcutcheon of ſtone, whereon three lions paſſant gardant are cut, with a lion paſſant gardant upon a helme, ſet on the corner of the ſhield, according to the faſhion of that time wherein he lived. This badge he fixed here in memory of King Henry the Second, the founder of this abbey. The annexed ſketch will give a general idea of this venerable fragment of antiquity, which is ſtill in perfect good condition. The following is a compendious account of the hiſtory of this abbey, and is thus given by Dugdale, " at " the time when the monaſtery was founded.

" There were, in the manour of Stonely, " ſixty-eight villains, beſides two prieſts; " alſo four bondmen, or ſervants, whereof " each

" each held one mefs, and one quartrone of
" land, by the fervices of making the gal-
" lows, and hanging of thieves; every one
" of which bondmen was to wear a red clout
" between his fhoulders, upon his upper gar-
" ment." After fpeaking of feveral of the abbots of the monaftery, Dugdale comments upon the conduct of one Thomas de Pipe, the then abbot, in the thirty-eighth of Edward the Third, with a merited degree of afperity. This fpiritual fuperior, to the great injury of thofe for whom he was entrufted, granted eftates to divers perfons for lives, without referving any rent whatfoever: and the fums for which thefe grants were made, are alledged to have been for the fupport of his concubine, Ifabella Beafhall, from whofe intercourfe with the holy father, there had, as report fays, proceeded images of his Maker, more in number than there were monks in the monaftery. He farther remarks, that he was a man of notable parts in other refpects, and deferved very well of the houfe.

By the survey taken in the twenty-fixth year of Henry the Eighth, the revenue of this abbey was certified to be one hundred and fifty-one pounds, three shillings, and a penny. It was suppressed in the following year by act of parliament, at which time the monks were for the most part disposed of to other religious houses that then remained undissolved; and Thomas Tutbury, the then abbot, had a pension of twenty-three pounds per annum assigned to him during his life. Upon the dissolution it was granted, in the thirtieth year of Henry the Eighth, to Charles Brandon, Duke of Suffolk, and afterwards through several hands passed to Sir Thomas Leigh, Knight, alderman of London, in whose family it has continued ever since. The present possessor is the honorable Mrs. Leigh, sister to the late owner, Lord Leigh.

The situation of this abbey is truly beautiful; the Avon, winding before the house
at

at a proper diftance, fupplies the corn and fulling mills, whofe diftant found, aided by the rufhing waters falling from the ftream, contribute in no fmall degree to render a complete landfcape delicious to a reflecting and contemplative mind.

From this charming fpot, the river Avon, gliding through the park, winds its eafy courfe amidft the adjoining fertile meadows for a fpace of about a mile, till it reaches Chesford bridge, at which place we fhall take leave of its bank, to meditate on the noble ruins of the once magnificent Kenelworth caftle.

SECTION VI.

THE superb ruins of Kenelworth castle are about two miles from the bank of our Avon, and there are not to be found in this kingdom many such specimens of antient splendor and magnificence. This castle was built in 1120, by Geoffrey de Clinton, a Norman, who was Lord Chamberlain, and Treasurer to King Henry the First. From the many points in which this stupendous pile may be viewed, and viewed to advantage, I have selected the annexed sketch, as comprising the most extensive assemblage of objects capable of giving a general idea of its consequence. It presents an internal view of the north front, including the great gate house, built by Lord Leicester; through the center of which the grand entrance was formerly made, under a spacious arch

arch that is now walled in. This building contains two large rooms on the ground floor, one of which is wainscotted with oak, taken from that part of the castle called Leicester's buildings. In this apartment is a spacious chimney piece of alabaster, with the armorial bearings, motto, and crest of the family, fancifully displayed in no indifferent style of sculpture. The great central building in the view is what is called Cæsar's Tower, which, though the most antient, is by much the strongest and most perfect part of these venerable ruins. Three sides of the walls yet remain nearly entire; the fourth was destroyed in the time of the civil wars, a period, the principles and energies of which contributed, in no small degree, towards bringing to a juster level the cloud-capt ambition of these towering palaces, and their loftier inhabitants. The walls of this tower are in many parts sixteen feet thick. The building to the left is called

called Leicester buildings, which, though the most modern erection, is yet approaching nearest to decay. This may in some measure arise from the brown and perishable stone of which it is constructed, but principally from the depredations that have been made on it, for the sake of the materials, which have either been applied in raising new buildings, or in repairing the roads in the neighbourhood.

EXTENSIVE and magnificent as these ruins appear to be, and interesting as they certainly are, to the curious observer, they yet fail in fixing determinately the eye of the artist, which is constantly wandering, and knows not where to rest, but fancies a thousand beautiful combinations for a picture, that, when attempted to be put on paper, are found to want something necessary towards producing a true picturesque effect. The main objects are too much scattered and

and broken to form one general mass or combination that may strike, and the whole pile wants due elevation to give it pictorial expression. The country around is likewise flat and uninteresting; yet, with all its disadvantages, the mind is so captivated by the surrounding features of the landscape, that it knows not how to quit this fascinating scene. Under this impulse, I made several other attempts to sketch these noble remains in various points of view; but they all fell so short of the general idea I entertained of the place, that I desisted, and was determined to rest on the one prefixed to this section.

The view which comprises Cæsar's tower and Leicester buildings, cannot, by the curious traveller, be passed unnoticed; the latter is overgrown with shrubs and ivy, in a form peculiarly diversified, and presents an object highly picturesque

and

and romantic. The splendid remain of the grand banquetting hall in Leicester buildings, is eighty-six feet in length, and forty-five in width. Beneath one of the windows, in the outer part of this building, is affixed a flat stone, on which appears the date 1571. This hall constituted the principal part, in point of magnificence, of this once stately mansion. The venerable Gothic groined arches, and beautiful antique fragments, the lofty and once stately windows, now fallen to decay, cannot but yield a melancholy sensation to the contemplative mind, suggesting the flow but sure decay of human greatness, and the futility of every object on which the pride of man seems to depend.

In this temper of mind let us turn our thoughts to the once flourishing state of this ruin, in the baronial reign of our Elizabeth. At that period we find it recorded, in a letter written

written by one Langham, an attendant of the court and who was prefent at the entertainment given at Kenelworth caftle by the Earl of Leicefter to the Queen, during her fummer's progrefs in 1579. In the quaint ftyle of the times, it runs thus:
" Who that confiderz untoo the ftately feat
" of Kenelwoorth caftl, the rare beauty of
" bilding that his honor hath avaunced; all
" of the hard quarry ftone: every room fo
" fpacioous, fo well belighted, and fo hye
" roofed within: fo feemly too fight by due
" proportion without: a day time on every
" fide fo glittering by glaffes; a nights, by
" continuall brightneffe of candel, fyre,
" and torch-light, tranfparent thro' lyght-
" fom wyndoz, az it wear the *Egiptian*
" *Pharos* relucent unto all the *Alexandrian*
" coaft: or els (too talke merily with my
" mery freend), thus radiaunt, az thoogh
" Phœbus for hiz eaz woold reft him in the
" caftle, and not every night fo to travel
" dooun

" dooun untoo the *Antipodes.* Heertoo fo
" fully furnifht of rich apparell and uten-
" filez apted in all pointes to the beft."

Her Majefty's introduction to the caftle has fomething fo truly whimfical in it, that I cannot pafs it unnoticed. " Her
" Majeftie benignly accepting, paffed foorth
" untoo the next gate of the brayz, which
" for the length, largenes, and ufe (as well
" it may fo ferve), they call now the tylt-
" yard, whear a porter, tall perfon, big of
" lim, and ftearn of coountinance, wrapt alfo
" all in fylke, with a club and keiz of quan-
" titee according, had a rough fpeech full of
" paffions in meeter aptly made to the pur-
" pofe: whearby (as her Highnes was cum
" within his warde) hee burft out in a great
" pang of impatiens to fee fuch uncooth
" trudging too and fro, fuch riding in and
" out, with fuch dyn and noiz of talk with-
" in the charge of his offis: whearof hee
" never

" never faw the like, nor had any warning
" afore, ne yet coold make too himfelf any
" cauze of the matter: at laft upon better
" vieu and avifement, az hee preaft too cum
" neerar, confeffing auon that he found
" himfelf pearced at the prezens of a per-
" fonage fo evidently expreffing an heroical
" foveraintee over all the whole eftates, and
" by degreez thear befyde, callm'd his fto-
" niz, proclaims open gates and free paffage
" to all, yeelds up his club, his keyz, his
" office and all, and on his knees humbly
" prayz pardon of hiz ignorauns and impa-
" ceens: which her Highnefs gracioullie
" graunting, he cauz'd hie trumpetoourz
" that ftood upon the wall of the gate thear,
" too fooound up a tune of welcuin."

FROM this grand hall the north paffage leads to the garden, or, as it was antiently called, the Plaifance. This fpot, containing an acre, or more, and joined to the park by a bridge,

bridge, is thus described by the same writer:
" The left arm of the pool, northward, has
" my Lord adorned with a beautiful brace-
" let of a fair timbred bridge, fourteen feet
" wide, and six hundred feet long, railed on
" both sides, and strongly planted, with
" a spacious terrace extending along the
" castle wall ten feet high, and twelve
" broad." Of this garden no traces are
remaining. A capacious lake formerly surrounded the southern, western, and part
of the northern walls of the castle: it is now
nearly dried up, and in a state little suited to
the representation of those splendid pagean-
tries which the same old author tells us were
exhibited by her favourite Leicester to Elizabeth. " The lady of the lake (famous
" in King Arthurz book), with too nymphes
" waiting her Highness comming: from the
" midst of the pool, whear, upon a moovabl
" *island*, bright blazing with torches, she
" floting to land, - met her Majestie with
" a well

" a well penned meeter and matter after this
" sort, (viz.) Firſt of the anncientee of the
" *caſtle*, who had been ownerz of the fame
" e'en 'till this day, moſt alweys in the hands
" of the Earle of Leyceſter; hoow ſhee
" had kept this lake finz King *Arthurz*
" days; and now underſtanding of her
" Highneſs hither cumming, thought it
" both office and duetie, in humble wize to
" diſcover her and her eſtate; offering up
" the fame, her lake and poowr therein,
" with promife of repayre unto the coourt.
" It pleaſed her Highneſs too thank this
" lady, and too add withall, we had thought
" indeed the lake had been oourz, and doo
" you call it yourz now? Well, we will
" herein commun more with yoo here-
" after.

" This pageant was cloz'd up with a
" harmony of hautboiz, ſhalmz, cornets,
" and ſuch oother looud muzik, that held
" on

" on while her Majeſtie pleaſauntly ſo
" paſſed from thence toward the *caſtl* gate;
" whereunto from the baze coourt over a
" dry valley caſt into a good foorm, waz
" thear framed a fayr bridge of a twenty foot
" wide, and a ſeaventy foot long, graveld for
" treading, railed on either part with ſeaven
" poſts on a ſide, that ſtood a twelve foot a
" ſunder, thickned betweene with well pro-
" portioned pillars turn'd."

At this ſtrange and whimſical entertainment, yet perhaps the moſt ſumptuous that ever was offered by a ſubject to his ſovereign, we find a Captain Cox appears to have been no inconſiderable actor; he is deſcribed, by Langham, as an " od man, by profeſſion a
" maſon, and that right ſkilfull and with
" great overſight in matters of ſtorie."
His library of romantic and humorous books is there mentioned, and is of ſuch a length as almoſt to diſturb the peace, at leaſt to ſet an
itching

itching the fingers of our black letter collectors, "Then," says our author, "he
"could talk az much in an afternoon
"without book az any inholder betwixt
"Brainford and Bagshot, what degree
"foever he be. Besides thiz, in the field a
"good marshall at musters; of very great
"credite and truft in the toun here; for he
"haz been chozen aleconner many a year,
"when his betterz have ftood by; and ever
"quitted himfelf with fuch eftimation, az
"yet too taft of a cup of nippitate; hiz
"judgment will be taken above the reft
"in the parifh, be hiz noze near fo read:

"Captain Cox cam marching on fo valiantly
"before, cleen truft and gartered
"above the knee, all frefh in a velvet cap
"(Mafter Golding a lent it him), floorifh-
"ing with hiz ton fwoord; and another
"fens mafter with him: thus in the forward
"making room for the reft. After
"them,

"them, proudly prickt on formoſt the
"Daniſh launce Knights on hoſbak, and
"then the Engliſh:" after which tilting
enſues, in which the Danes had twice the
better, but in the end are victorious.

WE have ſaid thus much of Captain
Cox, as he appears to have been a perſon of
ſuch notoriety in the time of Ben Johnſon,
as to render him a fit ſubject for his pen
fifty years afterwards; for in his Maſque
of Owls, at Kenelworth, preſented by the
ghoſt of our hero mounted on his hobby
horſe, he ſays,

> This captain Cox, by St. Mary,
> Was at Bullen with King Hary;
> And (if ſome do not vary)
> Had a goodly library,
> By which he was diſcerned
> To be one of the learned
> To entertain the Queen here
> When laſt ſhe was ſeen here.

And for the town of Coventry
To act for her sovereignty.
And for his sake the play
Was call'd for the second day.

ADJOINING to the church of Kenelworth stood the monastery, founded about the same period with that of the castle, and by the same Geoffrey de Clinton, from whom it had large endowments and privileges: they were no less than a tenth part of all the eatables that were brought into the castle; a right to fish in his pool at Kenelworth with boats and nets one day in every week; together with all his lamb skins throughout every his manours, as well those as should be killed to eat, as of others that might die casually.

OF this priory little remains but a fragment of the wall, which is sufficient to denote its former extent. Part of the chapel, and a venerable ruin of the old priory gateway, called,

called, I know not why, Tantarra, is annexed in the following sketch.

Of this Gothic entrance there remains sufficient yet to give pleasure to the eye of the antiquary, and to recommend it to general notice. Within the last two months, in digging in this vicinity, some valuable fragments of the foundation have been discovered, and, apparently, part of an aisle, or probably a cloister, appertaining to the abbey; the ornaments of the pillars, with their bases and capitals, appear to have been in a good style of Gothic architecture, and are scattered round the ground that has been dug up; but this discovery does not appear to have been taken up with that avidity which might be expected to attend a learned and curious pursuit, but seems rather to have been the effect of accident, and is not likely to be pursued to the extent which such vestiges of antiquity would have well warranted.

We shall now quit these venerable walls and returning to Chesford bridge, resume the subject of the Avon. This bridge is an antient stone structure of two circular arches. Though at the distance of eight miles from Combe abbey, it was formerly kept in repair by the abbot of that religious house, and is still preserved from dilapidation by Lord Craven,

Craven, the prefent owner of the abbey. From hence the river gently winds its courfe towards Blakefdown mill, a diftance of about a mile. Adjoining to the miller's fequestered retreat, which is overgrown with vines and ivy, is a handfome bridge; through part of which the reftrained water from the adjoining ftream falls in a gentle cafcade into the Avon. This beautiful fcene, heightened by the lengthening fhadows, reflected on the bofom of our river by a glowing evening fun, prefents one of the moft fimply elegant forms of landfcape that has occurred in purfuing the various windings of its banks,

"And foothes with many a penfive pleafure mild."

FROM the reflections that would naturally fuggeft themfelves to a contemplative mind in a retreat fo calm and tranquil as to give the image of genuine and truly philofolosophical happiness, one might be led to ask why man should with such eager and restless ambition busy himself so often in the smoke and bustle of populous cities, and lose his independence and too often his peace in the pursuit of a phantom which almost eludes his grasp—little thinking that with the accumulation of wealth he must create imaginary wants, under which perhaps that wealth melts away as certainly as under the more ready inlet of inordinate passion happiness is sacrificed.

The valleys through which the Avon pursues its meandering course after passing this charming scene, increase in richness, and verdure, and the country on the other side is beautifully screened by the luxuriancy of the neighbouring hills, on one of which the village and church of Hill-Wootton agreeably meets the eye, and gives additional lustre luftre to the fcenery. Approaching Guy's Cliff the admirer of elegant nature cannot avoid being ftruck with the happy combination of objects that prefent themfelves. From the annexed fketch the reader will beft form his judgment of the merit of the felection.

THIS charming fpot is the property and refidence of Mr. Greatheed whofe fuperior tafte, and claffic mind, is happily formed for the enjoyment of this elegant retreat of which Leland fays in his Itinerary, made in the time of Henry the Eighth, that it is a houfe of pleafure, a place meet for the Mufes,

"Nec non folitudo et quies Mufis amiciffima."

GUY'S CLIFF is fituated on the weftern bank of the river Avon. Dugdale fays "it "was made choice of by that pious man
"St.

"St. Dubritius (who in the Britons time
" had his epifcopal feat at Warwick,) for a
" place of devotion, where he built an ora-
" tory, dedicated to St. Mary Magdalen;
" unto which, long after, in the Saxon
" dayes, did a devout hermite repair; who,
" finding the natural rock fo proper for his
" cell, and the pleafant grove, wherewith it
" is backed yielding entertainment fit for
" folitude, feated himfelf here. Which
" advantages invited alfo the famous Guy,
" (fometimes Earl of Warwick) after his
" noble atchievements, having weaned him-
" felf from the deceitful pleafures of this
" world, to retire hither; where receiving
" ghoftly comfort from that heremite, he
" abode till his death. The ftory of his
" dwelling on this fpot is thus defcribed
" in the antient Ballade in the legend of
" Sir Guy."

" At

" At length to Warwick I did come,
 " Like Pilgrim poor, and was not known;
" And then I lived a Hermite life
 " A mile and more out of the Towne.

" Where with my hands I hewed a house
 " Out of a craggy rocke of stone;
" And lived like a Palmer poore
 " Within that Cave myself alone:

" And daily came to beg my bread
 " Of Philis at my Castle gate;
" Not known unto my loving wife,
 " Who daily mourned for her mate.

" Till at the last I fell sore sicke,
 " Yea sick so sore that I must die:
" I sent to her a ringe of golde,
 " By which she knew me presentlye.

" Then she repairing to the Cave
 " Before that I gave up the Ghost;
" Herself clos'd up my dying Eyes:
 " My Philis fair whom I lov'd most.

" Then

" Then dreadful Death did me arreſt,
 " To bring my corpes unto the grave;
" And like a Palmer dyed I,
 " Whereby I fought my life to fave.

" My body that endured this toyle,
 " Though now it be confumed to mould;
" My ſtatue faire engraven in ſtone,
 " In Warwick ſtill you may behold."

The ſtatue, here alluded to as being in Warwick, now ſtands at the ſouth end of the chapel in Guy's cliff, which was built by order of the before mentioned Richard Beauchamp, Earl of Warwick, who by his will ordained " that the old " chapel ſhould be new built, the coſt of " which, with the confecration of the two " altars, as appears by his executors from " the twenty-eighth to the thirty-ſeventh of " Henry the Sixth, was one hundred and " eighty-four pounds and five pence." This chapel is in perfect repair, but is not now uſed as a place of worſhip.

WE cannot pafs this antient ftatue without giving fome defcription of it: it is about eight feet high, and is very much mutilated. The annexed fketch will give fome idea of its prefent appearance, which is very different to that in Hollar's print, introduced in Dugdale, where it feems to be in a perfect ftate.

THE outfide of the venerable chapel, together

ther with part of the adjoining cliff, I likewise thought fit to give in the following sketch. The higher aperture in the cliff opens to a cave, said to have been the oratory of the famous Guy, and before it was the favourite walk of his lady, the fair Phillis, alluded to in the ballad before mentioned. She was the daughter of a Saxon Earl, Rohand, in the days of King Alfred; whose name was Felicia.

THIS place was the residence of another hermit,

hermit, one Thomas de Lewes, in the eighth of Edward the Third; and, after him, of one John Burry, in the tenth of Henry the Fourth, who had one hundred shillings per annum to pray for the good estate of Richard Beauchamp, then Earl of Warwick.

We must not omit to mention a celebrated inhabitant of this cliff, John Rous, the famous antiquary, who, after quitting the university, became a chantry priest in the chapel of this place, where he compiled his Chron. de Regibus, so often quoted by Dugdale, who, in his History of Warwickshire, has given a portrait of him by Hollar. He was buried in the church of St. Mary, Warwick.

In this cliff is formed, by a range of excavations, good stabling for horses, cellars, and out offices for the dwelling house, which are perfectly dry and wholesome. The cave

cave within this cliff that appears in the view prefixed to this section, produces a remarkable fine spring of water, which bears the name of Guy's spring. This spring rises through a small aperture in the solid rock; a part of which, containing two circular basons about eighteen inches diameter, is left standing in the middle of the grotto, being two feet in height from the level of the floor, and totally covered with a most beautifully verdant moss, about two inches in depth, and so thickly set as to vie in softness with the richest carpet.—The following lines are peculiarly appropriate:

> Intus aquæ dulces vivoque sedilia saxo,
> Nympharum domus.——

THE story of Guy, Earl of Warwick, is too generally known to bear repetition; Dugdale's relation seems to give it a degree of credibility, but we are inclined to think with Camden, that, besides its being fraught with

with much abfurdity, and that the days of chivalry, and their heroes, are now on the decline, the ftory is too much obfcured by fable and romance to obtain the leaft degree of credit.

DUGDALE fays that King Henry the Fifth, being at Warwick, vifited this place; but whether from refpect to the famous Guy, or to view "the rarenefs of the fitua-" tion," does not appear; and that he determined to have founded a chantry of two priefts, had he not been prevented by death: this purpofe was however accomplifhed by Richard Beauchamp, Earl of Warwick, in the firft year of Henry the Sixth.

THE Avon, winding round this romantic cliff, wafhes the foot of a large rock about a mile below it, adjoining to which a very extenfive mill is recently erected for the purpofes of grinding corn, and fpinning cotton;

it

it is called, from the adjacent quarry, Rock Mill. Here our Avon receives the aid of the river Leam, which rises near Braunston, in Northamptonshire. This river gives the name of Lemington to a village about two miles from the Avon; where, very near the bank of the Leam, rises a spring of water, of so saline a quality as, in Dugdale's time, to have been used for salting provision. A little below this is Emscote bridge, a very antient structure, and of great extent, which is rendered necessary from the immense swell of water in the adjoining meadows during the winter season.

SECTION VII.

About half a mile below Emſcote bridge the eye is gratified with an extenſive view of Warwick town, the venerable caſtle, and the new bridge recently built by the Earl of Warwick. Our Avon, gently winding through the extenſive meadows before us, paſſes under this ſimple and elegant arch, through the highly ornamented grounds of its noble owner. This ſpacious bridge conſiſts but of one arch formed of the ſegment of a circle, the diameter of which is 105 feet; its breadth 36 feet: the immenſe quantity of ſtone, uſed for building this bridge, was brought from the quarry at Rock Mill, mentioned in the cloſe of the laſt ſection: It was conſtructed by William Ebroal a maſon of Warwick who is recently dead but whoſe name deſerves to be recorded in this page not only as an artist but in the superior character of an honest and respectable man. The high road over it leads to Banbury, Daventry, &c. and is more commodious, and considerably nearer than the old one. This erection was made at a very great expence and solely at the charge of the noble Earl, who has applied it to the public use in lieu of the old one that crosses the river close to the foundation of his castle. This antient Gothic bridge is greatly in decay, and extremely narrow considered as a public road, yet, as a picturesque object united with the castle, must be acceptable to the eye of the connoisseur. From the acknowledged taste and munificence of its owner there is little reason to doubt but that it will long be preserved, not only as a public accommodation, but as a noble addition to the scenery of this venerable and stupendous castle.

THIS

This immense pile of building, considered in every point of view, affords matter of astonishment to the curious, and to render ample justice to its sublimity would require a volume of designs. A work of this nature, with a copious history of its origin, would be highly gratifying to the antiquary, and could not fail to be esteemed an accession to the arts even in the present æra of their refinement in this country. I shall in the present undertaking select two of the most prominent and striking features of this vast and stately building and such as were best adapted to the size of this volume and calculated to convey to the reader the clearest idea of this immense mass which, at the first *coup d' œuil* appears to be more than a mere work of art.

The annexed view is taken from the grand entrance, which lies in a north-east direction. By an easy ascent, through a spacious area of verdant lawns and shrubbery, we are led to contemplate this assemblage of embattled turrets, and aspiring towers. That on the right, is denominated Guy's, the other on the left Cæsar's Tower: the immense foundation of the latter appears behind the easy slope that rises to the grand gateway. This entrance stands on an arch thrown across the fosse over which was formerly a drawbridge. The foundation of this vast pile is raised on a prodigious rock, rising perpendicularly on the bank of our Avon, and the superstructure seems to be so connected with its base, that it appears rather to have grown out of it, than to have been artificially produced. The rock is known to run seventy feet below the surface of the earth, and, from appearances, there is reason to conjecture that it may penetrate still much deeper. The groined arches, excavated from this rock beneath the main building, are all, with great care and labor,

cased

cased with stone and are used as domestic offices to the castle. At what precise period this building was begun to be erected, historians seem not clearly to ascertain. Dugdale is doubtful whether to attribute its origin to Cymbeline, King of Britain, or to the Romans who had a strong hold or fortress at this place.

WARWICK was a Roman station on the fosse way, about fifteen miles from the station at Brinklow noticed before. The high artificial mount of earth is the Prætorium, and is visible from that at Brinklow, which is likewise visible from the Specula at Tripontium, a circumstance that, no doubt but the Romans availed themselves of when they kept our ancestors in subjection. Warwick, it is well known, was called by them Præsidium.

IN nine hundred and fifteen, Dugdale says, the

the renowned lady Ethelftede, daughter to king Alfred, certainly caufed the dungeon to be made, which was a ftrong tower or platform upon a large and high mount of earth, artificially raifed, the fubftance whereof is yet to be feen. The view of this tower in Dugdale, is delineated by Hollar, as ftanding at the weft end of the caftle: at that time caftles in this country were not very numerous, of which William the Conqueror was fo well aware, that he " neglected not to raife ftore of fuch " forts throughout the realm:" in the number of thefe, this at Warwick was not the leaft, and it appears that four houfes, then belonging to the monks of Coventry, were appropriated to the enlargement of it, and one Turchill de Warwick employed by the King to fuperintend the work; William however would not truft him with the cuftody thereof, but committed it to Henry de Newburgh, whom he advanced to the earldom

dom of Warwick. This caftle, towards the latter end of the reign of king Stephen, was delivered up by Gundred, the then countefs of Warwick, to Henry duke of Normandy, afterwards Henry the Second, on his arrival in this country. It was then committed to Hugh de Nevill, and, in the eighteenth of king John, unto Henry the then Earl of Warwick; at which period its confequence ftood fo high in the eftimation of the king, that, by his precept to the archbifhop of York, he requires good fecurity of Margery, fifter and heir to Thomas the then earl, that fhe fhould not take to hufband any perfon in whom the king could not repofe truft as in himfelf.

The hiftory of Guy's Tower, that appears in the preceding view, Dugdale gives in the following words. " The great tower
" at the north-eaft corner called Guy's
" tower the walls whereof are ten feet thick
" was

" was built by Thomas Earl of Warwick,
" about the 17th of Richard the Second, on
" whose banishment the custody of it was
" granted to John de Clinton, and in a short
" time after to Thomas Holland, Earl of
" Kent." In the reign of Henry the Fourth it reverted to its former possessor, the Earl of Warwick, nor does it appear, from that time till the reign of Edward the Fourth, to have been out of the hands of the succeeding Earls of that family. On the death of George Duke of Clarence, it was seized by the King, during the minority of his son Edward Plantagenet, and from this time continued in the hands of the crown, till the first of Edward the Sixth, when John Dudley was advanced to the Earldom of Warwick: on his attainder, in the first of Mary, it escheated to the crown, till restored by Elizabeth to one of his sons Ambrose and his heirs, whom she likewise created Earl of Warwick: he dying without issue, it

came

came again to the crown, and was, by King James in the second year of his reign, granted in fee to Sir Fulk Greville Knight, afterwards created a Baron in the eighteenth year of this reign, by the title of Lord Brooke, Baron Brooke, of Beauchamp-court, in the county of Warwick: at this period the castle was in a very ruinous state, and the strongest parts of it were used as a common goal. This Lord Brooke says Dugdale, " bestowed more than 20,000l. cost in re-
" pairing and adorning it, and made it a
" place, not only of great strength, but ex-
" traordinary delight, with most pleasant
" gardens, walls, and thickets, such as this
" part of England can hardly parallel; so
" that now it is the most princely seat that
" is within these midland parts of this
" realm."

SPEED, after mentioning the extraordinary expence bestowed in repairs upon the castle

castle by this learned and great man, pays him an unreserved tribute of gratitude for his kind patronage in rescuing him from the mechanical employment to which he had been originally destined. "His merit to "me-ward I do acknowlege in setting this "hand free from the daily employments of "a manual trade, and giving it full liberty "thus to express the inclination of my "mind, himself being the procurer of my "estate." To enumerate the high and amiable qualities of this great man, who gloried in having been the friend of Sir Philip Sydney, would be foreign to this work; we shall content ourselves with having had the honor of introducing a name that must ever be held dear to this country, and of observing that its lustre is not diminished by descent. The grand area, or inner court of the castle, has an air of solemn magnificence, that is superior to any thing of the kind I have yet seen: The many additions that have

have been made by the present Earl are so analogous to its original design as to render it an honor to the taste of its owner. The interior apartments are uniformly splendid, and so judiciously suited to domestic uses, as to erase from the mind of a stranger, every idea of its ever having been a castle of defence; and leave him wholly in admiration of the beauty, and magnificence of a place, once celebrated only for its strength. The collection of pictures, particularly the works of Rembrandt, Rubens, and Van Dyck, are highly deserving the attention of the connoisseur; they were all purchased by the present Earl, whose superior knowledge of the fine arts is not less evinced by works of his own pencil than by this judicious selection. The various scenes that present themselves from the different apartments of the castle are noble and extensive; the Avon beneath, rendered by art a capacious river, winds its course through a rich and highly cultivated park castle by this learned and great man, pays him an unreserved tribute of gratitude for his kind patronage in rescuing him from the mechanical employment to which he had been originally destined. " His merit to " me-ward I do acknowlege in setting this " hand free from the daily employments of " a manual trade, and giving it full liberty " thus to express the inclination of my " mind, himself being the procurer of my " estate." To enumerate the high and amiable qualities of this great man, who gloried in having been the friend of Sir Philip Sydney, would be foreign to this work; we shall content ourselves with having had the honor of introducing a name that must ever be held dear to this country, and of observing that its lustre is not diminished by descent. The grand area, or inner court of the castle, has an air of solemn magnificence, that is superior to any thing of the kind I have yet seen: The many additions that

have

have been made by the present Earl are so analogous to its original design as to render it an honor to the taste of its owner. The interior apartments are uniformly splendid, and so judiciously suited to domestic uses, as to erase from the mind of a stranger, every idea of its ever having been a castle of defence; and leave him wholly in admiration of the beauty, and magnificence of a place, once celebrated only for its strength. The collection of pictures, particularly the works of Rembrandt, Rubens, and Van Dyck, are highly deserving the attention of the connoisseur; they were all purchased by the present Earl, whose superior knowledge of the fine arts is not less evinced by works of his own pencil than by this judicious selection. The various scenes that present themselves from the different apartments of the castle are noble and extensive; the Avon beneath, rendered by art a capacious river, winds its course through a rich and highly cultivated park for a space of near two miles, when it happily breaks upon the eye, in different points of view, emulous as it were to enrich this luxuriant scene.

We shall now quit the internal part of the castle, and, to give a more full idea of its situation, attempt a general view of its grand south and west fronts, as they appear from the new bridge before mentioned. Here the extent of this noble building is viewed in its utmost perfection. The judicious alterations that have been, and are still making to the windows, in the southern front, by giving them a Gothic form, adds much to their picturesque appearance; and Guy's stately tower, although its immense rocky base is lost to the eye in that point of view, is yet an object highly worthy of admiration. This view, taken altogether, though on a small scale, will yet, I flatter myself, give a faithful picture of this principal

cipal ornament of our Avon, on whose delightful banks we shall for a short time suspend our comments, to make some cursory observations on the antient town of Warwick, which stands on a rocky eminence, and in a dry and fertile soil. Dugdale says, " it was the chiefest " town of these parts, and whereof the " whole county upon the first division of " these realms into shires took its name, " so may it justly glory in its situation " beyond any other." This town contains many objects that render it worthy notice, the first of these is, pre-eminently, the Lady's Chapel, in the church of Saint Mary; which is one of the most beautiful specimens of the rich Gothic style I remember to have seen. We are sorry to add, that in a recent repair made to this once venerable building, so much attention has been paid to its former gilding, and gaudy decorations, that it now glares so much on the eye as to produce

duce a disgusting effect. We are not however without a hope that it may one day be restored to its primitive simplicity and elegance.

In this chapel are some splendid monuments, particularly one in the centre, of Richard Beauchamp, Earl of Warwick; who lies on a tomb of marble. The figure is of brass, double gilt, and is surrounded by many images in the same metal. On a monument erected in this chapel, to the memory of a lady Leicester, who died on the morning of a Christmas day in 1634, are some lines which from the singularity of their style may not be thought unworthy transcribing. This lady's qualities according to Master Gervas Clifton the Poet's account, were really wonderful, she not only cast cannon, but multiplied the heavenly host, in courtly phrase we can say no less, that glitter around the throne, and

was

was at once a belle, an amazon, and a saint!

> " She, that did supply the Warrs
> " With thunder, and the Court with stars,
> " Thought it safest to retire
> " From all care, and vain desire.
> " And because she took delight
> " Christ's poor members to invite,
> " She fully now requites her love,
> " And sent his Angels from above
> " That did to Heaven her soul convey
> " To solemnize his own Birth-day."

THE collegiate church of St. Mary, which was rebuilt by Thomas Beauchamp, Earl of Warwick, in 1394, was destroyed by a dreadful conflagration in 1694, and no part left standing but the beautiful chapel of our lady before mentioned. In the year 1704, this church was rebuilt from a design of Sir Christopher Wren, which design we are sorry to say is in many parts very inferior to the general excellence of that great architect. To
cen-

censure any work of so distinguished an artist, may appear arrogant: his strong partiality for the Grecian and Roman style of design, in preference to the Gothic, is evident in all his works; and how judiciously soever he may in this point have decided, in the present undertaking he has most absurdly, and I doubt not but that the public opinion will accord with mine, blended together the inferior and discarded ornaments of each without either sense or meaning. This jumble is no where more palpable than in the forms of the windows, where a double row of cumbrous circular, or Saxon arches, are terminated above by such grotesque and barbarous forms, as to baffle all conjecture as to what order or country they could belong. In other parts of this large building will be found many inconsistencies, which we are the more surprised at, as he had before him the elegant chapel above alluded to, and which he could not but be aware must remain as a part

of

of this vast edifice. Within this church a very judicious alteration, that of removing the organ from the centre of the building to the west end, is now carrying into execution. The custom of placing the organ in the former situation, so universally prevalent, is matter of astonishment to those who are capable of feeling the full effect of beautiful symmetry in the works of architecture: by this barbarism in taste, the sublime interest, we take in the

" Long drawn aisle and fretted vault"

of our Gothic cathedrals is in a great degree destroyed; and the most striking and impressive works of human invention obscured by a range of gilded pipes, that can only be entitled to a secondary consideration.

In foreign churches this instrument, how respectable soever, holds only its due and subordinate station, and is usually placed between

tween the pillars at the side of the grand aisle.

As an architect of considerable taste and skill, Warwick has to boast the name of Hiorne, a native of this place. The gate at the east end of the town is from his design, as well as the new gaol and church at the lower part of it. They have each a claim to their respective merits, and those considerable, although placed in the vicinity of two of the grandest works in the kingdom, the castle and the chapel of our lady in the church of St. Mary before mentioned.

QUITTING this handsome town, we shall return to the bank of our Avon, which, in its course through the richly diversified grounds belonging to Warwick castle, acquires in some places a breadth of not less than two hundred feet, and no where less than one hundred. Its depth is full twelve feet,

feet, having an excellent found and gravelly bed, which it retains for the diſtance of upwards of two miles and a half in and below the park. Paſſing down the river, the ſpacious green-houſe, recently built by the preſent Earl, and deſigned by William Eboral before mentioned, ſtands on a riſing lawn, and agreeably meets the eye at a proper diſtance from its margin. Within this building is placed a vaſe of exquiſite workmanſhip, in white marble, brought by his Lordſhip from Tivoli. This ineſtimable ſpecimen of Grecian ſculpture was diſcovered ſome years ſince near Adrian's villa there; it is in a high ſtate of preſervation, and in its deſign and execution, beautiful beyond conception. Three different engravings of it will be found in Piraneſe's views.

WITH the beautiful curve of the river the eye is highly gratified, nor leſs ſo with the luxuriant plantations ariſing in each direction,

rection, under the auspices and taste of their noble owner, who, fully aware that elegance in landscape is not to be produced without space, has unremittingly embraced every occasion that offered towards completing this bold enterprize. The various productions of the fir, larch, and other trees, that have been raised in these grounds within these few years, give ample proof of the richness and excellence of the soil, nor should the cedar of Lebanon be forgotten as the produce of these grounds, which has yielded some thousands within the last twelve or fourteen years.

Towards the middle of the park, by turning a high road into another direction, the Earl has caused to be made a spacious lake of water, from ten to twenty feet deep, from a small stream which issues at Chesterton, in this county, about six miles distant. This water is between three and four hundred feet wide,

and

and extends about a mile in length; it is capable of being continued near two miles farther within this spacious park.

PASSING the keeper's lodge, which stands on a confiderable eminence on the bank of the river, a new intereft is created in the mind of the difcerning traveller, by a retrofpective view of the caftle; which, at the clofe of day, lofing the nice difcrimination of its minuter parts, melts into one grand and general mafs of light and fhade: nor is the fcenery, looking down the river, lefs gratifying. Here the Ilmington hills, which bound our view with the intervening villages, aided by the winding of the Avon in the fore ground, form altogether a richly variegated landfcape.

WE cannot quit this park without noticing another handfome ftone bridge of one arch, ten feet wide, thrown acrofs the Avon, which

which being left unfinished by the late Earl, was completed about seventeen years since by the present. At the extremity of the park on the southern bank of the river, we pass the village of Barford, where a new bridge is now erecting, to supply the place of the old one, which by length of time had fallen to decay. We find nothing here worthy notice; but, as Camden has thought proper to advert to a story of rather a singular nature respecting this place, we shall here transcribe it. He says, " that in 1647, one Samuel Fairfax
" was born at this place, who, at twelve
" years old, dwelt under the same roof, and
" eat at the same table with his father and
" mother, grandfather and grandmother,
" great grandfather and great grandmother;
" who all lived very happily together: and
" none of the three generations of either
" sex had been twice married." Neither the longevity, nor domestic happiness of this extraordinary family, could avert the ill fortune

tune that purfued the laft male branch of it to Warwick gaol a few years fince; where he lingered and died for a debt contracted by a fhopkeeper in his village, for whom he was furety. A little below Barford, the Avon receives the tributary aid of a rapid though fmall ftream, called the Sherbourne, which paffes, in its courfe, a pleafant village fo called, from whence we prefume it derives its name. Here, through a fine and fertile champaign country, our river directs its courfe by Wafperton to Fulbroke.

On a confiderable eminence called Caftle Hill, formerly ftood Fulbroke caftle, faid to have been built by John, Duke of Bedford, third fon to Henry the Fourth, regent of France. This caftle was taken down in the reign of Henry the Eighth, by Sir William Compton, Knt. who had then the cuftody of the park. After it was pulled down, the materials were conveyed to Compton Wy-
niate,

niate, from which Sir William erected the edifice now standing.

On this spot formerly stood the seat of the Earls of Northampton.

About two years since, some vestiges of the foundation of Fulbroke castle were accidentally discovered by a boy in raking the ground, which was then sown with oats. These were a brick vault with stone steps, nearly filled up with earth, and some fragments of Gothic stone windows. It does not appear that the castle was ever finished.

The adjoining park, which had been antiently in the possession of Sir Francis Englefield, was, in the time of our immortal Shakspeare, in that of the Lucys, who had been long settled in the neighbouring village of Charlecot. It was in this park our bard is said to have been, in a youthful frolic, engaged

The deep and lofty woods, the lawns and walks of this park, scenes that, in tempers less apt, naturally prompt and invite to musings and heavenly contemplation, were doubtless the haunts of his early youth; and to his rambles in these coverts and recesses it is more than probable that we are indebted for those exquisitely passionate reflexions upon the sufferings and fate of that noble and beautiful animal, the Deer. In tracing the progress of its strugglings, and miseries, down to its mortal catastrophe under the savage and deliberate butchery of the huntsman, how unquestionable soever the warrant which puts the life of animals in the disposal of man, humanity is by this powerful appeal made to recoil at the abuse, and shudder at least at the mode in which the warrant is carried into execution against a fellow creature.

SUGGESTED in the spot of which we are speaking, the following lines, which the most fastidious would hardly think out of place any where, will, we trust, be thought fit accompaniments to this scene. Entitled, as they are, to a regard in adamant, and living, as they ought,

" In the heart's core, aye, in the heart of hearts,"

their immortality can in no degree depend on the frail memorial of these humble pages. We pay no more than a passing tribute of respect.

" *Duke.* Come, shall we go and kill us venison?
" And yet it irks me, the poor dappled fools,
" Being native burghers of this desart city,
" Should in their own confines, with forked heads
" Have their round haunches gor'd.

" *1st Lord.* Indeed, my lord,
" The melancholy Jaques grieves at that,
" And, in that kind, swears you do more usurp
" Than doth your brother that hath banish'd you:
" To-day my Lord of Amiens, and myself
" Did steal behind him, as he lay along
" Under an oak, whose antique root peeps out
                                          " Upon

" Upon the brook that brawls along this wood;
" To the which place a poor sequester'd stag,
" That from the hunter's aim had ta'en a hurt,
" Did come to languish; and, indeed, my lord,
" The wretched animal heav'd forth such groans,
" That their discharge did stretch his leathern coat
" Almost to bursting; and the big round tears
" Cours'd one another down his innocent nose
" In piteous chase; and thus the hairy fool,
" Much mark'd of the melancholy Jaques,
" Stood on th' extremest verge of the swift brook,
" Augmenting it with tears."

SECTION VIII.

QUITTING Fulbroke and Hampton wood, on the western bank of the Avon, we pass the pleasant village formerly denominated Bishop's Hampton, now Hampton Lucy. It derives this name from the antient family of the Lucy's at Charlecot on the opposite side of the Avon, which near this place receives the aid of Thelesford brook. The venerable mansion, as given in the annexed view, is neither so picturesque nor perfect in its Gothic parts, as the grand front on the opposite side, it is, yet, selected as comprizing a view of the river; an advantage that could not be obtained in any other point of observation. This house was built by Sir Thomas Lucy, Knight, in the first year of Queen Elizabeth's reign. It is of brick, with stone coins, and still makes a venerable appearance, although it has, in many

many parts, particularly in the forms of the windows, been modernized. The grand front at the entrance is nearly in its original ftate; and the great outer-gate, the inner part of which is feen in the annexed view, is a handfome fpecimen of the Gothic ftyle ufed at the period of its erection. As I do not remember to have feen any view of this manfion, the fketch it is prefumed, will not be unacceptable to the reader. The Lucy family boafts a very antient and noble defcent, but perhaps have not, by any of their high connections or military achievements, acquired more celebrity than from the reputation of having profecuted our divine bard Shakfpeare, for ftealing deer out of the park at Fulbroke, as mentioned at the clofe of the laft fection. The ftory, although well known, is yet fo materially connected with the prefent undertaking, that I may be permitted to give it, as recorded on the authority of Mr. Rowe;

who

who, in his account of the life of our Bard, says, "Shakſpeare, by a misfortune com-
"mon enough to young fellows, had fallen
"into ill company; and amongſt them,
"ſome, that had made a frequent practice
"of deer-ſtealing, engaged him, more than
"once in robbing a park belonging to Sir
"Thomas Lucy, of Charlecot, near Strat-
"ford. For this he was proſecuted by that
"gentleman, as he thought ſomewhat too
"ſeverely; and in order to revenge that ill
"uſage, he made a ballad upon him. And
"though this, probably the firſt eſſay of
"his poetry, be loſt, yet it is ſaid to have
"been ſo very bitter, that it redoubled the
"proſecution againſt him to that degree,
"that he was obliged to leave his buſineſs
"and family in Warwickſhire for ſome
"time, and ſhelter himſelf in London."
The loſs of the ballad, here alluded to, we cannot ſufficiently regret: we have however in the Merry Wives of Windſor, under the

X cha-

character of Juſtice Shallow, ſtrong marks of the bard's reſentment, and from what cauſe ſoever it ſprung, a degree of acrimony beyond the mere ridicule and contempt, which the vanity and ignorance of a booby Juſtice might be ſuppoſed to provoke. The temper with which he wrote will be beſt ſeen in his own words on the occaſion. Juſtice Shallow, in his ſpeech to Sir Hugh Evans, alluding to Falſtaff, who is repreſented as having ſtolen the deer, ſays, " I " will make a Star chamber matter of it : " If he were twenty Sir John Falſtaff's, he " ſhall not abuſe Robert Shallow, Eſq.

" *Slender.* In the county of Gloſter, Juſtice of Peace " and coram.

" *Shallow.* Ay, couſin Slender, and Cuſt-alorum.

" *Slender.* Ay, and ratolorum too; and a gentleman " born maſter parſon; who writes himſelf armigero; in " any bill, warrant, quittance, or obligation, armigero.

" *Shallow.* Ay, that I do; and have done any time theſe " three hundred years.

" *Slen.*

"*Slen.* All his succeffors, gone before him, have done't; and all his anceftors, that come after him, may; they may give the dozen white luces in their coat.

"*Shallow.* It is an old coat.

"*Evans.* The dozen white loufes do become an old coat well; it agrees well, paffant: It is a familiar beaft to man, and fignifies love.

"*Shallow.* The luce is the frefh fifh; the falt fifh is an old coat.

"*Slender.* I may quarter, Coz.

"*Shallow.* You may, by marrying.

"*Evans.* It is marring indeed if he quarter it.

"*Shallow.* Not a whit.

"*Evans.* Yes, py'r-lady; if he has a quarter of your coat, there is but three fkirts for yourfelf, in my fimple conjectures: but that is all one: If Sir John Falftaff have committed difparagements unto you, I am of the Church, and will be glad to do my benevolence, to make atonements, and compromifes between you."

THE three hundred years, mentioned by Shallow, evidently refer to the antiquity of the Lucy family, whofe pedigree is deduced by Dugdale, from the reign of Richard the Firft, a period of about four hundred years before the play was written; but the family did not

not take the name of Lucy, till the 34th of Henry the Third, which corresponds nearly with the period above stated. The arms of the family are clearly pointed at, when Slender speaks of the dozen white Luces in their coat. The armorial bearings are three Luces hauriant, between nine crofs croslets, on a field *Or*. Lucius is a Latin name, though of no good authority, for the fish called Jack or Pike, with which species of fish the Avon abounds near this spot, and they are commonly called Luces. In the kitchen of this mansion is a portrait of a pike, caught in this river in the year 1640, which weighed forty pounds.

In the church at Charlecot are several handsome monuments of the Lucy family; the earliest of which is that of Sir Thomas Lucy, who built the family mansion, and was the supposed prosecutor of our Bard; as I do not remember to have seen a portrait of him, I have here annexed ed an etching of the head, as taken from the monumental effigies, and which will convey some idea of the man, as far as the likeness may be supposed correct, which, from the masterly style of its execution, may very reasonably be inferred. He died on the 18th of August, 1600. No portrait of him remains in the mansion house, nor can I learn that there is any extant. It is somewhat singular that on this monument there should not be found any memorial of the Knight himself, even so slight as to give the year in which he died, or the age which he had then attained; though there appears a strong testimonial to the excellent character of his lady, who lies by his side, and who died at the age of sixty-three, written and signed by himself. Whether it is not modish at present for husbands to speak in such exalted terms of their wives, or whatever may be the character of modern wedlock, the pleasure we receive in recording the virtues and excellencies of the

sex,

sex, particularly in a married state, is a sufficient inducement to make the following extract. The Knight, after many other honorable testimonies, concludes with this culogium: "When all is spoken that can be "said, a woman so furnished and garnished "with vertue as not to be bettered, and "hardly to be equalled by any. As she "lived most vertuously, so she dyed most "godly. Set down by him that best did "know what hath been written to be "true.

"THOMAS LUCY."

AT Charlecot the Avon receives the aid of a small river called the Heile, that rises in Northamptonshire, and in its course passes near Kyneton, Compton, and through Welsburn, in this neighbourhood. About a mile lower, on the south, it likewise receives a small stream called Littleham brook, where the parish of Alverstone begins; a place, the

the air of which is considered as being so pure and falubrious, that it was called by the late learned Dr. Perry, The Montpelier of England. From hence the river winding its pleasant course, affords a beautiful and extensive view of the Feldon of Warwickshire, called the Vale of Red Horse. This rich and fertile scenery is interspersed with extensive woods, rising out of a verdant champaign country, and its vast amphitheatre is bounded by a range of azure hills, forming a beautiful and undulating line; amongst these, Edge hills proudly distinguish themselves at a distance of about twelve miles.

We cannot pass these memorable hills although at such a distance without adverting to the famous battle fought there between the King and Parliament army in 1642. The King left Shrewsbury with about 10,000 men directing his course towards the capital under a full determination to give battle to the

the Parliament army as soon as possible. Essex who had received his instructions two days after the Royalists had quitted Shrewsbury, left Worcester, and strange and incredible as it may appear, the two armies had marched ten days in utter ignorance of each other's motions or situation, and were within six miles of meeting ere either of the generals was acquainted with the approach of his adversary. The day was far advanced when the King determined on the attack, in which the degree of success he obtained, seems to have been principally owing to the conduct of Sir Faithful Fortescue, who, having been obliged to serve in the parliament army, soon after the engagement took place, ordered his troop to discharge their pistols in the ground and then put himself under the command of Prince Rupert. After a heavy conflict and various success the fortune of the day does not seem to have been decided, nor can it be said, that

that victory declared herself absolutely for either party in the shock of battle, as the two armies faced each other for a considerable time, without having confidence to renew the onset. The best title, which the Royalists have to the claim which they make of the victory is derived from a fact that is unquestionable; that Essex, the Parliament General left the field of battle in possession of the royal army. The King did not attempt to harrass the retreating army, but soon after retired into quarters.

There were 5000 men left dead on the field, of whom there appears to have been an equal number slain on both sides.

Amongst those who in that most calamitous and melancholy contest with a true spirit of heroism shed their blood in support of the principles they reciprocally held sacred,

it

it would be injuftice not to draw into more general notice one, who, ranging himfelf under the royal ftandard, in that memorable day made himfelf eminently confpicuous.

THIS gentleman was a Dr. Lake, a civilian, the anceftor of the prefent Sir James Lake, Bart. and the perfon from whofe merits and whofe fufferings that family derives its hereditary honours. From a love of his fovereign, and a full conviction of the juftice of his caufe, the Doctor, laying afide the gown, took up the fword and followed his royal mafter to the battle of Edge hill. In this engagement he received fixteen wounds; and having loft his right hand, he placed his horfe's bridle between his teeth and boldly held out the combat, fighting with his fword in his left hand till the armies parted. The friendly and affectionate part taken by the amiable, though ill-advifed, and unfortunate monarch, in the concerns of this loyal fubject

ject and very gallant adherent, is of so very marked and curious, as well as interesting a nature, that I here transcribe the history of it, by favour of Sir James Lake, from the original manuscript in the Doctor's own hand writing, which has never before been made public.

"After I had made my escape from
" my imprisonment at Mr. Bent's, at Corsby,
" where I was kept seven weeks after the
" battell at Edghill, I went to Bangor, in
" Carnarvonshire, in Christmas, 1642.
" Thence I writ to Dr. Steward, the Clerk
" of the Closett at Oxford, certifieing him
" in what condition I was, and of the hurts
" I received at Edghill, and hee sent back to
" me to send him up the certificate thereof
" under the chirurgion's hand, which after-
" wards I did, under the hands of Mr. John
" Angel, the physitian, and Mr. Edward
" Lufman, the chirurgion, both of Leicester,
" who

" who were emploied upon my cure. The
" next yeare, about a fortnight after
" Michaelmas, I went out of Wales towards
" Oxford, where I came about the 20th of
" October, 1643.

" Dr. Steward wifhed me not to come
" into the King's prefence till the 23d day of
" that month, the anniverfary day of Edghill,
" which hee faid the King intended to keep
" folemnly, with publique thankfgiving for
" the victory on that day. And that day,
" a little before dinner, in the prefence
" chamber at Chriftchurch, I kift his Ma-
" jeftie's hand, Dr. Steward being with mee;
" who faid to his Majeftie, as I was goeing
" to kifs his hands, Sir, this day twelve-
" months the Doctor was in another cafe
" (Dr. Steward having formerly, as he told
" me, fhewed his Majeftie that certificate of
" my hurts received at Edghill). His Ma-
" jeftie looking upon me, faid, *It is true you*
" *loft*

" *lost a great deall of blood for mee that daie,*
" *and I shall not forgett it, but you shall bee re-*
" *membered for it, both by way of armory, and*
" *otherwise.* Then looking upon Dr. Steward,
" and others standing by, said, *For a lawyer,*
" *a professed lawyer, to throw off his gown and*
" *fight so heartily for mee, I must needs think*
" *very well of it.*

" I HUMBLY thanked his Majestie for
" his gracious acceptance of my poore endea-
" vours to serve him, and praised God for
" preserving mee for further service to his
" Majestie, to the best of my power, ac-
" cording to my bounden duties; *and,*
" *Doctor* (said the King, bending his head a
" little towards me), *I have reason to believe*
" *it,* and so went into the privie chamber.
" About two months after, his Majestie
" sent mee to Worcester, then garrisoned by
" Sir Gilbert Gerrard, the King's governor
" there, to whom his Majestie writt; which
" letter

" letter thou haſt, ſignifying to him the
" loſſe of my eſtate in England, and Ire-
" land, by the rebellion, and ſixteen wounds
" I received at the battel at Edghill. With
" this letter, about the beginning of Chriſt-
" mas, I went down to Worceſter, and
" taking my leave of Dr. Steward, hee
" (whether his Majeſtie had, when he ſign-
" ed that letter, or at other time, ſpoken
" him hereof, I know not, but probably he
" had), aſked mee whether I had drawn up
" that note, touching an addition in armo-
" rie, which the King ſaid he would give
" mee, when I kiſs'd his hands on the an-
" niverſary day of Edghill. I told him I
" had done nothing therein; he bad mee
" adviſe with ſome herald thereupon, and
" draw up a note to that purpoſe for the
" King to ſigne, and to leave it with him.

" I DID hereupon adviſe with Sir Wm.
" Le Neve, but did not acquaint him with
" the

" the King's words touching armorie; and
" after I had talked with him, I drew up
" such a note for his Majestie's signature,
" mentioning onely that coat of augmen-
" tation (without any mention of one of the
" lions of England), and the crest. This
" note I left with Dr. Steward; and, the
" next somer, his Majestie coming to Wor-
" cester, and Dr. Steward with him, Dr.
" Steward gave me this docquett, signed by
" his Majestie, and attested by the Doctor,
" touching the baronetshipp, and arms.
" Of which addition of one of the lions of
" England in the coat of augmentation, and
" besides to have the nomination of a Ba-
" ronett, and to be a Baronett myself, being
" altogether beyond my expectation, I asked
" the Doctor the reason thereof; hee told
" mee, that presently upon my goeing
" from Oxford to Worcester, hee shewed
" his Majestie that note for the coat of aug-
" mentation, which I left with him. His
" Majestie

" Majeſtie read it, and ſaid, *I deſerved more;*
" *and ſhould have more; I ſhould have one of*
" *his own lions too, and I ſhould have the making*
" *of a Baronett, and that I ſhould bee a Baro-*
" *nett myſelf;* and his Majeſtie himſelf, with
" his own hand, interlined ſome words in
" that note touching the bearing of that
" lion, and for the nomination of a Baro-
" nett, and the creation of mee to bee a Ba-
" ronet, and bad the Doctor bring it to
" him, written more at large; whereupon
" the Doctor, within a daie or two after,
" brought it written, as it is here, to his
" Majeſtie, which hee ſigned, and ſaid to
" him, *Doctor, you ſhall bee Secretary for this*
" *buſineſs; ſett your hand to it, and witneſs my*
" *ſignature; and tell Dr. Lake, that hee may*
" *keep this a while by him, and not take out the*
" *patent, till I ſhall better provide for him.*
" And the ſame day, at Worceſter, as be-
" fore, when Dr. Steward had told mee this,
" which was at the Lord Biſhopp's palace,

at

"at Worcester, I went with him into the presence, and there kissed his Majestie's hand, who said to me, thus, *the Doctor there* (looking at Dr. Steward), *I suppose has told you my minde.* I said, Yes, Sir; and most humbly thanked his Majestie for his exceeding favours to me; then his Majestie beeing, it seemed, in hast upon businefs, went out of the Psence, and as hee was going, lookt back towards mee, and beckoned to me, and I made my address to him, who said thus to mee, *Doctor, if you will, you may keep that a while by you* (meaning that aforesaid docquet), *and not take out the patent, till I shall better provide for you, which I hope I shall doe ere long;* and so he went away, and I kept this by mee, as thou seest."

BELOW Alveſtone, to the south of the Avon, Welcombe hills, and lodge, the seat of George Lloyd, Esq. are seen in the most

favour-

favourable point of view. These hills have been anciently the scene of warm contests between the Britons and Saxons. The vast entrenchments, known by the name of Dingles, which were made by the latter, are yet evident. These Dingles, or Dells, are formed from large excavations made in the earth, sometimes forty or fifty feet deep: they were deemed a sufficient defence against the force of any warlike engines then in use, and from their pointed forms, may not improperly be called Double Angles.

WELCOMBE hills are apparently the work of art, and probably were thrown up by the soldiers, after their battles, in memory, as well as for cover, of entombing their slain.

AMONG the Northen people, Camden observes, that every surviving soldier, after a battle, was forced to bring his proportion of earth

earth towards raifing a monument for his comrades flain on the fpot.

WELCOMBE belonged to the Combe family, till the beginning of the prefent century, fince which period, having paffed through feveral hands, it was purchafed by John Lloyd, Efq. father of the prefent poffeffor.

FROM hence the Avon, in a winding direction, conducts us to Stratford bridge, on the fouthern extremity of which ftands the antient manor houfe of the parifh of Alveftone.

SECTION IX.

THE approach to Stratford upon Avon presents to our view a venerable stone bridge of fourteen Gothic arches. It is walled on each side, and at the western extremity of it has an extensive causey. On the centre of this bridge is a stone pillar, at the top of which are cut the arms of the city of London, and below these are the armorial bearings of the Clopton family. The following lines are inscribed under the arms:

Sir Hugh Clopton, Knight,
Lord Mayor of London, built this bridge
At his own proper expence;
In the reign of King Henry the Seventh.

SIR HUGH was likewise Sheriff of London in the reign of Richard the Third.

The river Avon was made navigable from Tewkesbury to this place in 1637, by a Mr. Sands. The town of Stratford is by Dugdale traced into so high and remote antiquity as three hundred years before the Norman conquest, at which time it belonged to the bishopric of Worcester.

In the seventh year of the reign of Richard the First, this town obtained a weekly market, by means of John de Constanciis, then Bishop of Worcester. Richard likewise bestowed on the burgesses of this town the inheritance of their burgages, paying yearly for each of them to himself and his successors twelve pence for all services at the four great feasts of the year, and that they should be free of toll for ever, according to the custom of Bristol.

In the sixteenth year of King John, they obtained a charter for an annual fair, which was

was to commence on the eve of the holy Trinity, in honour of which myſtery the church of Stratford had been dedicated. Fairs were antiently held on Sundays, a cuſtom frequently inveighed againſt by the clergy of thoſe times, as productive of great immorality; but their admonitions ſeem to have had little effect till towards the latter end of the reign of Henry the Sixth, when all merchandize, except the produce of the harveſt that was exhibited for ſale on Sundays or holidays, was forfeited to the lord of the liberty or franchiſe. The keeping of wakes was alſo, under antient uſages, an annual feſtival, held on the Saint's day to whoſe memory the church was dedicated, and thence called the feaſt of dedication. The depraved uſes made of theſe wakes are well deſcribed in an old legend of St. John the Baptiſt; the ſubſtance of which Dugdale ſays he found engliſhed in an old manuſcript as follows (black letter): " And ye ſhall underſtand and
" know

" know how the *Evyns* were furſt found in
" old time.

" In the beginning of holi chirche with
" candellys brennyng and wold *Wake*, and
" coome with light toward night to the
" chirche in their devocions; and after they
" fell to lecherie and ſongs, daunſes, harp-
" ing, piping, and alſo to glotony and ſinne,
" and ſo tourned the holineſſe to curſydnes:
" wherefore holy faders ordeined the pepull
" to leve that *Waking*, and to faſt the *Evyn*.
" But hit is called *Vigilia*, that is *Waking* in
" Engliſh, and it is called the *Evyn* they
" were wont to come to chirche."

To whatever conſequences they may lead
—to whatever licence our preſent wakes
may give birth, it affords ſome degree of
ſatisfaction to the ſerious and reflecting
mind, that the abuſe is no longer practiſed
under the cloak and ſanction of religion.

THE

THE entrance to the town of Stratford acrofs the meadow partakes neither of the beautiful or picturefque; the buildings are mean, and the adjoining fcenery flat and uninterefting: but looking to the left, the eye is gratified with a pleafing view of the venerable church of Stratford rifing on the margin of our gentle Avon. In the chancel are enfhrined the facred remains of our immortal bard, who in this town, as is well known, firft drew breath, firft received his truly infpired gift,

" The pomp and prodigality of heaven;"

and unlefs it muft be allowed that a partial view has fometimes been opened to Milton, had to him alone that myfterious veil withdrawn by nature, who has fince

" Curtain'd clofe fuch fcenes from every future view."

Though not with equal genius, we tread this fairy scene with equal reverence, and with as true devotion, as was breathed by the late Mr. Thomas Warton, in the following elegant and well imagined lines:

" Whom on the winding Avon's willow'd banks
" Fair fancy found, and bore the smiling babe
" To a close cavern: (still the shepherds shew
" The sacred place, whence with religious awe
" They hear, returning from the field at eve,
" Strange whisp'ring of sweet music through the air.)
" Here, as with honey gather'd from the rock,
" She fed the little prattler, and with songs
" Oft sooth'd his wond'ring ears, with deep delight
" On her soft lap he sat, and caught the sounds."

Upon entering the town of Stratford, a feeling, I trust, something more elevated than that of mere curiosity, naturally directs the steps of every admirer of our divine Poet towards that spot which gave birth to the most extraordinary genius this or any other country

country has ever produced: of whom Ben Jonson, a rival wit and a contemporary, nobly says,

> "Triumph, my Britain! thou haft one to shew,
> "To whom all scenes of Europe homage owe.
> "He was not of an age, but for all time;
> "And all the Muses still were in their prime,
> "When like Apollo he came forth to warm
> "Our ears, or like a Mercury to charm.
> "Nature herself was proud of his designs,
> "And joy'd to wear the dressing of his lines."

As it is avowedly the intention of this work to give pictorial representations of objects that may in any degree illustrate either the history or biography of our country, it must be with peculiar pleasure that we lay before the public the representation of any thing that is nearly connected with the life and history of our matchless Bard. As such we shall conduct them to the humble cottage in which

which he first drew breath, on the 23d of April, 1564.

The annexed sketch of it was made in October, 1792.

Part of these premises, which belonged to Shakspeare, are still occupied by a descendant of Joan Harte, sister to our Poet, who pursues

pursues the humble occupation of a butcher. His father, Thomas Harte, died about a year ago, at the age of sixty-seven. He informed me, that, when a boy, he well remembered having, with other boys, dressed themselves as Scaramouches (such was his phrase) in the wearing apparel of our Shakspeare.

The kitchen of this house has an appearance sufficiently interesting to command a place in this work, abstracted from its claim to notice as a relative to the Bard. It is a subject very similar to those that so frequently employed the rare talents of Oslade, and therefore cannot be deemed unworthy the pencil of an inferior artist. In the corner of the chimney stood an old oak chair, which had for a number of years received nearly as many adorers as the celebrated shrine of the Lady of Loretto. This relic was purchased in July, 1790, by the Princess Czartoryska, who made a journey to this place, in order to obtain

tain intelligence relative to Shakspeare; and being told he had often sat in this chair, she placed herself in it, and expressed an ardent wish to become a purchaser; but being informed that it was not to be sold at any price, she left a handsome gratuity to old Mrs. Harte, and left the place with apparent regret. About four months after, the anxiety of the Princess could no longer be withheld, and her secretary was dispatched express, as the fit agent, to purchase this treasure at any rate: the sum of twenty guineas was the price fixed on, and the secretary, and chair, with a proper certificate of its authenticity on stamped paper, set off in a chaise for London.

PART of the premises adjoining is, and has been many years, occupied as a public house, known by the sign of the Swan and Maidenhead. Our Bard, it appears by the Register of Stratford, was the eldest son of John

John Shakſpeare, a conſiderable dealer in wool. Were his origin queſtionable, the above evidence, and correſponding tradition receives a degree of confirmation from a pane of glaſs, taken out of one of the windows of this houſe, about thirty years ago, by Mr. Peyton, who then kept the White Lion inn adjoining.

On this glaſs is painted the arms of the merchants of the wool ſtaple; and I have

have little doubt, from the ftyle of its execution, but that it was painted at or before the time of John Shakfpeare, the father. The pane of glafs is about fix inches in diameter, and very perfect. The preceding fketch is a faithful reprefentation of the original in the poffeffion of Mr. Peyton of Stratford, fon of the before mentioned gentleman.

In a lower room of the public houfe, which is part of the premifes wherein Shakfpeare was born, is a curious antient ornament over the chimney, relieved in plaifter, which, from the date 1606 that was originally marked on it, was probably put up at the time, and poffibly by the poet himfelf: although a rude attempt at hiftoric reprefentation, I have yet thought it worth copying, as it has, I believe, paffed unnoticed by the multitude of vifitors that have been on this fpot, or at leaft has never been made public:

public: and to me it was enough that it held a conspicuous place in the dwelling house of one who is himself the ornament and pride of the island he inhabited. In 1759, it was repaired and painted in a variety of colours by the old Mr. Thomas Harte before mentioned, who assured me the motto then round it had been in the old black letter, and dated 1606. The motto runs thus:

"Golith comes with sword and spear,
"And David with a sling;
"Although Golith rage and sweare,
"Down David doth him bring."

These premises appear, by some long timbers still remaining across the building, to have included two houses adjoining: indeed it does not seem possible that there could have been sufficient space in one of these cottages to have reared a family of ten children, the number that John Shakspeare the father is said to have had, nor would it have been suited to a person of his situation in life, who, we are told by the register and public writings relative to the town of Stratford, was of a family of good figure and fashion there, and therein mentioned as gentlemen. It likewise appears that he had been a corporation officer and bailiff of Stratford, and that he enjoyed some hereditary lands and tenements, the reward of his great grandfather's faithful and approved service to King Henry the Seventh. In the year 1599, John Shakspeare, in honour of his son, took out an extract of his family arms from the herald's office. Still, how re-

respectable soever the family may have been, there remains little doubt but that these humble premises were in their occupation. As a corroborating proof of this fact, if any is necessary, I shall give the substance of a family settlement in my possession, dated August 14th, thirty-third of Elizabeth, 1591, which describes the house of John Shakspeare as situated in Henley Street. It is to this effect; "That George Badger, senior, of Strat-
"ford upon Avon, conveys to John and
"William Courte, yeomen, and their heirs,
"in trust, &c. a messuage or tenement,
"with the appurtenances, in Stratford upon
"Avon, in a certain streete called Henley
"Streete, between the house of Robert
"Johnson on the one part, and the house
"of *John Shakspeare* on the other; and also
"two selions (i. e. ridges, or ground between
"furrows) of land lying between the land of
"*Thomas Combe*, Gent. on the one hand, and
"Thomas Raynolde, Gent. on the other."

It is regularly executed, and livery of seisin on the 29th of the same month and year indorsed.

The Thomas Combe above mentioned was most probably the brother of the celebrated John. Thomas was buried, according to the Stratford register, January 22d, 1609-10. The land adjoining, occupied by him, came, I presume, at his death, to his brother John, and was most likely that spot called Shakspeare's Close, bequeathed by him to his brother George, by his will dated 1614.

Our Shakspeare, we have every reason to believe, was educated at the free grammar-school which stands over the Guildhall at Stratford, and is introduced in the annexed view. Its external appearance, except that it has been whited and painted, remains nearly in its antient form. Within it is a
large

large unfurnished chamber, probably at that time the school room. The old chapel adjoining, erected in Henry the VII.'s reign, by Sir Hugh Clopton, who built Stratford bridge, likewise remains in its primitive state. To make, therefore, the representation of the contemporary scene, so far as it has reference to our Bard, entire, I have taken the liberty of giving a view of the house as it stood at the time he resided there, which he did from the period of his quitting London till his death. The view is copied from an old drawing of one Robert Trefwell's, made in 1599, by order of Sir George Carew, afterwards Baron Carew, of Clopton, and Earl of Totnefs. It was found in Clopton house in 1786, and was in the possession of the late Mrs. Patriche, who was the last of the antient family of the Cloptons. The drawing, I am informed, is since lost or destroyed. The site on which the house stood is now a garden, in the possession of Thomas Hunt,

Hunt, Esq. A wall is standing next the street, which ascertains the exact width and situation of the front of the house. By the appearance of the drawing, the house was of brick, with stone coins. It was built by Sir Hugh Clopton, a younger brother of the antient family of that name, who built the bridge at the entrance of the town. He particularly bequeaths it, by will, to his nephew, by the appellation of his Great House in Stratford. It had been alienated from the family of the Cloptons for more than a century when Shakspeare purchased it; and this was, in all probability, about four or five years before his death, according to the opinion of Theobald and Rowe. When Shakspeare had made a purchase of these premises, he thoroughly repaired them, and gave them the name of New Place. Soon afterwards, in 1614, two years before his death, the greater part of the town of Stratford was destroyed by fire, but this

this houfe fortunately efcaped the conflagration.

On the death of Shakfpeare, in 1616, this houfe continued in the poffeffion of his wife, who died in 1623, and then became the property of his favourite daughter, Sufannah, the wife of John Hall, a phyfician of fome eminence in the county. He died in 1635, and fhe in 1649, at the age of fixty-fix: it was, therefore, during the time in which fhe was the owner of New Place, that Henrietta Maria, Queen to Charles the Firft, kept her court here for three weeks. This event took place in 1643, the year in which the firft ferious, though indecifive appeal to arms was by her ill-fated hufband made at Edge Hill in this county. The Queen entered Stratford upon Avon in triumph, about the 22d of June, at the head of three thoufand foot, and fifteen hundred horfe, with a confiderable train of artillery. She accompanied thefe

thefe troops from Newark, which place they left on the 16th of June. The Queen was met at Stratford by Prince Rupert, who had alfo with him a large body of troops. From Stratford the Queen procceded to the plain of Keinton, under Edge Hill, to meet the King, and from thence, after the battle, they went to Oxford, at which place it is faid their

" Coming was rather to a triumph than a war."

AFTER the death of Mrs. Hall in 1649; I am informed the premifes were occupied by their daughter Elizabeth, who was firft married to Thomas Nafh, Efq. and afterwards to Sir John Bernard of Abbington. After the death of Lady Bernard, it was fold under her will to her coufin, Edward Nafh, from whom it devolved, in 1678, to Reginald Fofter, Efq. afterward Sir Reginald Fofter. Of this gentleman it was re-purchafed by the

the Clopton family, who soon after pulled down the house, and built another on the spot. The new one was occupied by a Sir Hugh Clopton, a barrister at law, who was knighted by King George the First. In the year 1742, this gentleman entertained Mr. Garrick, Mr. Macklin, and Mr. Delane, under Shakspeare's Mulberry Tree, then standing in the garden. The truth of the tradition that this tree was planted by our Bard, seems to admit of little doubt. In support of the fact, it appears that, in the beginning of the seventeenth century, this species of fruit tree being very scarce in England, King James the First ordered a considerable number of young ones to be imported from France, and to be planted in different parts of the country, in order to increase the quantity of silk worms, and to aid the manufactory of silks. This celebrated Mulberry Tree was cut down about fifty years ago, by one Gastrell, who then possessed the premises, and who committed this sacrilegious act merely to avoid the trouble of answering the earnest importunities of the frequent traveller, whose zeal might prompt him to hope that he might meet inspiration under its shade, and who could with confidence tell the proudest admirers of the most rapturous strains that ever echoed in the enchanted groves of the highly cultivated regions of Greece and Rome,

" Ne quis sit lucus, quo se plus jactet Apollo."
VIRGIL.

By the same irreverend hand was the house pulled down, about the year 1752, and for no other or better reason than a difference with the magistrates because they had assessed his house at Stratford, in which he resided only a part of the year, proportionably with all others in the borough: as the only means of defeating the effect of a determination every way

way reasonable and just, in a selfish and unfeeling spleen he rased the building to the ground.

The antient building opposite to New Place as described in the annexed plate, is a public house, known by the sign of the Falcon, and is evidently in the same state it was, in Shakspeare's time. It is built of upright oak timbers with plaister, and has all those Gothic ornaments that denote it of still more antient date than the period above alluded to. The sign, in all probability, was first set up as a compliment to Shakspeare, whose crest of cognisance, according to the instrument in the College of Heralds, was a Falcon with his wings displayed, standing on a wreath of his colours supporting a spear armed headed or steeled silver. Julius Shaw was the name of the person who then kept the house, and who was a subscribing witness to our Poet's will.

Shaw was by trade a carpenter and undertaker, and is supposed, with some degree of probability, the person who buried him. Shakspeare is said to have passed much time in this house, and to have had a strong partiality for the landlord, as well as for his liquor.

Upon the demolition of New Place above mentioned, all the furniture and papers were removed to the antient mansion of the Clopton family, about one mile distant from Stratford. Amongst those papers I have long imagined that it was very possible some manuscripts of our Shakspeare might have been conveyed. Prompted by a faint hope of this sort, as well as by curiosity, I last summer visited this spot, but without the desired success. Of this venerable house, with the church of Stratford in the distance, I have annexed a faithful sketch. It presents

sents an irregular front, built in the time of Henry the Seventh, the grand aspect has been modernized, and is in so indifferent a style as to be unworthy notice.

In Clopton house are a few antient pictures and curious old furniture; amongst the latter is a bed, given to Sir Hugh Clopton, who built the mansion, by Henry the Seventh, and in which he is said to have frequently slept. The furniture of this bed is of fine cloth of a darkish brown, with a rich fringe of silk about six inches deep. This remain of antiquity is in good preservation, and is annexed to the estate as an heir loom. The garret, or attic story of this house, was formerly used as a chapel, and on its walls yet remain several scriptural inscriptions in black letter, and paintings on religious subjects, that appear as antient as the house. Amongst other hieroglyphic figures,

is

is a large fish rudely designed, with a hand at a distance dragging it forward with a string. As a specimen of the poetry written on the walls, take the following:

"Whether you rise yearlye or goe to bed late,
"Remember Christ Jesus that died ffor your sake."

FROM this place I shall conduct the reader to the village of Shottery, about a mile from Stratford, from whence, as report says, our Bard, at about the age of seventeen, took to himself a wife aged twenty-four, named Anna Hatheraway, or Hathaway. The cottage in which she is said to have lived with her parents is yet standing, and although I have doubts as to the truth of the relation, I have yet given a faithful representation of it in the annexed view. It is still occupied by the descendants of her family, who are poor and numerous. To this same humble cottage I was referred when this house long before the time of Shakspeare.

The proprietor of this furniture, an old woman upwards of seventy, had slept in the bed from her childhood, and was always told it had been there ever since the house was built. Her absolute refusal to part with this bed at any price was one of the circumstances which led to a persuasion that I had not listened with too easy credulity to the tale she told me respecting the articles I had purchased. By the same person I was informed, that at the time of the Jubilee, the late George Garrick obtained from her a small inkstand, and a pair of fringed gloves, said to have been worn by Shakspeare.

Returning to Stratford we shall contemplate the venerable pile that received the remains of our immortal Poet,

"Whose sacred dust yon high arch'd aisles inclose,
"Where the tall windows rise in stately rows
"Above th' embowering shade."

PART of this respectable Gothic structure is said to have been built soon after the Conquest. The chantery was founded by John de Stratford, Bishop of Winchester, in the fifth of Edward the Third. The church was made collegiate by Henry the Sixth, under the name of the collegiate church of Stratford upon Avon. Its revenue was valued, at the Dissolution, at one hundred and twenty-nine pounds a year. On the north side of the chancel of this church is affixed the monument of Shakspeare, the view of which is faithfully represented in the annexed sketch. The figure of the bard, in stone, is beneath a circular arch: he holds a pen in his right hand, and his left is resting on a scroll of paper which lies on a cushion before him. This bust, though rudely sculp-

sculptured, is yet, I have little doubt, a resemblance of the man. Some likeness may certainly be traced between this and the print prefixed to the first folio copy; and for the authenticity of this point, we have Ben Jonson's testimony.

In the countenance of the late Mr. Thomas Harte, the descendant of Shakspeare's sister before mentioned, I always perceived a strong similitude to the markings of this figure. The monument has lately undergone a very judicious alteration, that of restoring it to its natural stone colour, and removing the various daubings by which it was defaced in attempting to give to the figure the representation of nature. Beneath the figure is the following distich :

" Judicio Pylium, genio Socratem, arte Maronem,
" Terra tegit, populus mœret, Olympus habet."

To this Latin inscription are added the following verses :

" Stay,

"Stay, paſſenger, why doſt thou go ſo faſt?
"Read, if thou canſt, whom envious death hath plac'd
"Within this monument; Shakſpeare, with whom
"Quick nature dy'd, whoſe name doth deck the tomb
"Far more than coſt; ſince all that he hath writ,
"Leaves living art but page to ſerve his wit."

OVER the grave, at the foot of this effigies, is placed a flat ſtone with another epitaph engraved, in the following uncouth manner, in ſmall and capital letters:

"Good Frend for Ieſus SAKE forbeare
"To digg T-E Duſt EncloAſed HERe
"Bleſe be ÞE Man Ɏ ſpares ÞEs Stones
"And curſt be He Ɏ moves my Bones."

THE Gothic door-way adjoining to this grave, and which appears in the print, opens to the charnel houſe, which contains the greateſt aſſemblage of human bones I ever ſaw. This ſolemn ſcene was peculiarly calculated to make a forcible impreſſion upon ſuch

such a mind as that of Shakspeare's, and may probably have given birth to that striking exclamation, at which, however just the image, and beautiful the composition, humanity almost recoils, and the soul thrills with horror.

" Chain me with roaring bears;
" Or shut me nightly in a Charnel house,
" O'er cover'd quite with dead mens ratling bones,
" With reaky shanks, and yellow chaples sculls,
" Things that to hear them told have made me tremble."

ON a grave-stone adjoining to Shakspeare's was formerly, according to Dugdale, the following inscription on Susannah, his favourite daughter, who married Dr. Hall. From the character given of her in her epitaph, she seems to have inherited no inconsiderable portion of her father's talent. It is penned with much quaintness, and is a curious, and at the same time by no means a contemptible
specimen

specimen of the character of the writings, and of the genius of the times. In nothing did the age of James improve upon Elizabeth: on the contrary, under him learning degenerated into pedantry, and simplicity fell a sacrifice to puerile conceit.

" Witty above her sexe, but that's not all,
" Wife to salvation was good Miſtris Hall,
" Something of Shakſpeare was in that, but this
" Wholy of him with whom ſhe's now in bliſſe,
" Then paſſenger ha'ſt ne'er a teare,
" To weep with her that wept with all;
" That wept yet ſet herſelfe to chere
" Them up with comforts cordiall.
" Her love ſhall live her mercy ſpread,
" When thou ha'ſt ne're a teare to ſhed."

SEVERAL other relatives of Shakſpeare's are interred in this vault; and very near his monument is that of John Combe, Eſq. an intimate acquaintance of our Bard. A well ſculptured figure in alabaſter of this gentle-man,

man, in a cumbent pofition, is placed beneath an arch over his grave; from which, as I do not remember to have feen a print I have made the annexed fketch. The infcription on his monument runs thus:

"Here lyeth interred the body of John
"Combe, Efq. who departing this life the
"tenth day of July, A. D. 1614, bequeathed
"by his laft will and teftament to pious
"charitable ufes thefe fummes enfuing, an-
"nually to be paid for ever, viz. xxs. for two
"fermons to be preach't in this church.
"vi. il, iiis, ivd, to buy ten gownes for ten
"poore people within the borough of Strat-
"ford; and one hundred pounds to be lent
"to xx. poore tradefmen of the fame bo-
"rough from three years to three years,
"changing the parties every third year at
"the rate of 50s. per annum; the which in-
"creafe he appointed to be diftributed to-
"wards

" wards the reliefe of the almes-poor there.
" More he gave to the poore of Stratford
" xxl.

" Virtus post funera vivit."

For the erection of this monument, he directs in his will that " a convenient " tomb of the value of threescore pounds " shall be by my executors within one year " set over me." This gentleman is said to have been famed for his wealth and usury, and from a well known story, told by Mr. Rowe, one is led to believe that Shakspeare, at the request of his friend John Combe, made the following extempore lines on him by way of epitaph:

" Ten in the hundred lies here ingrav'd,
" 'Tis a hundred to ten his soul is not sav'd;
" If any man ask, who lies in this tomb,
" Oh! oh! quoth the devil, 'tis my John-a-Combe."

We shall quote some other fustian lines on a similar subject, imputed to our Bard, and perhaps on still more slender authority, on one Tom a Combe, alias Thin-beard, brother to John, the gentleman before alluded to.

" Thin in beard, and thick in purse;
" Never man beloved worse;
" He went to the grave with many a curse:
" The devil and he had both one nurse."

The lines on John Combe are said to have been written after Shakspeare's retirement to Stratford, which must have been, according to Mr. Rowe, within one year of John's death: he died, at an advanced age, in 1614.

We find from the will of John Combe, that he " bequeathed unto Master William " Shakespeare five pounds." The witty lines written for his epitaph, were so bitter and pointed, that they would hardly have been by any one communicated to the object of their satire. King James is said to have expressed an anxious wish that he might survive the author of a satirical epitaph upon his minister Salisbury; and it seems not at all improbable that John, whose advanced years would not admit the hope of surviving Shakspeare, and who must know how far he was himself open to attack, might discreetly endeavour to conciliate him, by yielding a very small part of that, which he could not carry with him, as a peace offering, to secure the quiet and repose of his grave.

As it is our professed intention to remark on works of art in the present undertaking, we cannot pass the Town Hall without noticing the portrait of our late Roscius, David Garrick, who is there exhibited at full length,

length, in a picture copied from an original of the late ingenious Mr. Gainsborough. This picture exhibits a tolerably good likeness; yet as it could have no claim to a reception in this place, except from the faithful and eloquent manner in which he whom it represents reflected the various scenes of nature and workings of passion drawn by the pen of our mighty master of the drama, he ought not in our opinion to have been painted in the fashionable dress of the day. Being admitted as a public character, and a very distinguished one he certainly was; he ought to have had an habit appropriate. The blue coat and long skirted scarlet waistcoat, belaced with gold, gives rather the idea of a half-pay naval officer, than that of the idol of the public—of a genius, the magic of whose powers held throughout his life the passions of a nation under their controul—whose smile enlivened, and whose frown appalled and petrified. The portrait of Shakspeare, at the other end of the hall, is by the late Benjamin Wilson, and was painted in 1769. The attitude of the figure is well conceived, but wants sufficient animation in the colouring to produce effect: the face in particular is so much under shadow, that, if the features as truly indicate the powers, as they are said to do the passions, of the mind, the countenance is so far clouded as by no means to give the idea of that fire and spirit which one must suppose would be visibly emanating from the soul of its divine original. Without any model upon which to rest, it is perhaps imposing a heavy task upon the imagination to body forth the form of excellence; and though the picture has in many respects much merit, we cannot resist the temptation of applying our great author's own words, as they accord so much with our own feelings on this occasion:

" If

" If any such be here
" That love this painting wherein you see me smear'd,
" Let him express his disposition."

I CANNOT quit Stratford without adverting to the celebrated Jubilee held here in honour of Shakspeare, in September, 1769, under the conduct of the late Mr. Garrick. The annexed view of the grand Amphitheatre was presented to me by a friend, who was on the spot at the celebration of this classic fête. The procession of the characters in Shakspeare has been since added nearly as they were intended to have appeared, had the weather permitted. As I do not remember to have seen a correct view of this scene in print, it may not prove unpleasant to the admirers of our Bard.

THE Amphitheatre was an elegant octagon structure, erected at a small distance from the bank of the Avon, in the meadow adjoin-

adjoining to Stratford bridge, as described in the view at the opening of this section. It was, in point of size, not quite so large as Ranelagh, supported by a colonade of the Corinthian order, about ten feet distant from the sides of the building. In the centre was, suspended from the roof, a large chandelier, consisting of eight hundred lights. The building was handsomely decorated with paintings appropriated to the occasion, and between the pillars were crimson curtains elegantly disposed. This festivity was intended to be complete in three days. On the first, the company attended at the church, where the oratorio of Judith was performed under the conduct of Dr. Arne, its composer; after which the procession, with a band of music, led on by Mr. Garrick, proceeded to the hall, where the company dined and closed the evening with a masquerade ball. On the second day the grand procession of the principal characters in Shakspeare's plays was omitted, from the excessive exceffive rain, little fhort of a deluge, that poured down all the morning. The fketch annexed is therefore to be confidered rather as what was intended, than what was really exhibited.—It is not our defign to go into a more particular defcription of the hiftory of this Jubilee, nor to fpeak to the merits of the performance, the fubject is yet too recent in the minds of many who were prefent. We fhall therefore only hint at the pictorial reprefentations exhibited on that occafion.

FRONTING the building, on the bank of the Avon, were three well executed allegorical paintings, after the defigns of the late Sir Jofhua Reynolds. In the centre, Time was leading Shakfpeare to immortality, and on each fide a figure of Tragedy, and Comedy: behind thefe figures were placed a great number of lamps, which produced, from their tranfparency, a beautiful effect. In the five windows

windows of the Town Hall were likewife tranfparent paintings, on filk, of Lear, Falftaff, Piftol, Caliban, and the Genius of Shakfpeare, who is feizing on a figure that holds Pegafus, and who is in the attitude of exclaiming,

"Oh! for a Mufe of fire!"

Nor was the humble dwelling, where our Swan of Avon firft drew breath, left undecorated on this occafion: a tranfparent painting was hung before the windows of the room in which he was born, reprefenting the Sun breaking through a Cloud. His buft in the church was decorated with feftoons of laurel, bays, &c. and at one end of the grave-ftone fome pious hand had placed a garland of flowers, evergreens, &c.

Such was the enthufiafm of the vifitors at this voluntary national tribute of homage

to

to our immortal Bard; and such will ever be the extatic veneration with which every inhabitant of the globe to whom the English language is known, must contemplate this divine genius,

"Who (taught by none) did first impart
"To Fletcher wit, to labouring Jonson art:
"He, monarch-like, gave those his subjects law,
"And is that nature which they paint and draw.
"Fletcher reach'd that, which on his heights did grow,
"Whilst Jonson crept, and gather'd all below.
"This did his love, and this his mirth digest:
"One imitates him most, the other best.
"If they have since outwrit all other men,
"'Tis with the drops that fell from Shakspeare's pen."

SECTION X.

ABOUT a mile below Stratford, near Luddington, is the confluence of the river Stour with our Avon. From hence, on the south, we pass Milcot, anciently the seat of the Grevils. Of this mansion, except part of a moat which surrounds a farm house now standing on the site, scarce any traces remain. Below this is the village of Weston, in Gloucestershire, in whose church are interred many of the Grevil family. This place, together with the adjoining village of Welford, now belongs to the Duke of Dorset. The lock, adjacent mill, and contiguous scenery, afford no unpleasing landscape.

FROM hence, toward Bidford, about six miles, the Avon runs nearly in a direct line, without any material object to engage attention, till we reach Hillborough. Within this village stands a very antient house, on a pleasing ascent from the bank of the Avon, known by the appellation of Haunted Hillborough. It is now a farm house, and why it bears the epithet of haunted, we cannot learn; but as we shall shortly have occasion to refer to it, it is here mentioned. A little below this place is Bidford grange, a very antient house, formerly belonging to the monastery of Evesham, from whence it passed into the antient family of the Skipwiths, and is now the property of Lady Skipwith.

The country round about this charming spot, the mill house, and spacious water fall adjoining, on the bank of the Avon, form a scene truly picturesque, and of which the preceding view is a faithful representation.

This neighbourhood, so contiguous to Stratford, and so inviting in itself, was much
fre-

frequented by Shakfpeare; and this fpot may not improbably have laid the fcene as well as exhibited the picture of thofe ruftic manners, a copy of which forms the fimple paftoral trio between Autolycus, Mopfa, and Dorcas, in the Winter's Tale, when Mopfa fays,

" Or thou go'ft to the grange, or mill,
" *Dorcas.* If to either thou doft ill,
" *Aut.* Neither. *D.* What, Neither? *A.* Neither.
" *Dor.* Thou haft fworn my love to be;
" *Mop.* Thou haft fworn it more to me:
" Then whither go'ft? fay whither?"

BIDFORD was formerly a market town, but the market is now in difufe. It was antiently a demefne of the crown, poffeffed by King Edward the Confeffor, and retained by William the Conqueror. Bidford has little at prefent attached to its hiftory worth obfervation: the only circumftance that now gives it notoriety, is its excellent ale, and the equally notorious thirfty clay of its inhabitants. It is faid there were antiently two focieties of village yeomanry in this place,

place, who frequently met under the appellation of Bidford Topers. It was a custom with these heroes to challenge any of their neighbours, famed for the love of good ale, to a drunken combat: among others the people of Stratford were called out to a trial of strength, and in the number of their champions, as the traditional story runs, our Shakspeare, who forswore all thin potations, and addicted himself to ale as lustily as Falstaff to his sack, is said to have entered the lists. In confirmation of this tradition we find an epigram written by Sir Aston Cockayn, and published in his poems in 1658, p. 124: it runs thus:

" To Mr. Clement Fisher, of Wincot.

" *Shakspeare*, your *Wincot* ale hath much renown'd,
" That fox'd a beggar so (by chance was found
" Sleeping) that there needed not many a word
" To make him to believe he was a lord:
" But you affirm (and in it seems most eager)
" 'Twill make a lord as drunk as any beggar.
" Bid

treated him to return to Bidford and renew the charge; but this he declined, and looking round upon the adjoining villages, exclaimed, "No! I have had enough; I have
"drank with

> "Piping Pebworth, Dancing Marston,
> "Haunted Hillbro' Hungry Grafton,
> "Dudging Exhall, Papist Wicksford,
> "Beggarly Broom, and Drunken Bidford."

Of the truth of this story I have very little doubt: it is certain that the Crab Tree is known all round the country by the name of Shakspeare's Crab; and that the villages to which the allusion is made, all bear the epithets here given them: the people of Pebworth are still famed for their skill on the pipe and tabor: Hillborough is now called Haunted Hillborough; and Grafton is notorious for the poverty of its soil.

On the south side of the Avon, opposite to Bidford, lies the pleasant village of Barton,

ton, which is a hamlet belonging to the parish of Bidford. From the similarity of the name, and the consideration that no such place as *Burton* Heath has been by any enquiry of mine discovered in this neighbourhood, I am led to conceive that Barton Heath, which lies in this county, and is about eighteen miles from Stratford, must have been the spot to which Shakspeare refers in the first act of the Taming of the Shrew, where Sly says " Am not I Christopher Sly, old Sly's " son of *Burton* Heath ? Ask Marian Hacket, " the fat ale-wife of *Wincot*, if she know me " not. If she say I am not fourteen pence on " the score for sheer ale, score me up for the " lying'st knave in Christendom." I am not only fortified in this conjecture, but emboldened to make another, by the further consideration, that on Barton Heath there is a house yet standing formerly a public house, called Woncott or Onecott. Nothing is more common than to vary the mode of spelling the names of towns and of families in different periods.

periods. The above were doubtless places with which Shakspeare was very familiar. It is worth hazarding a conjecture to have even the chance of tracing him in any one of his haunts. Right or wrong in that, which we have hazarded (and in this age what has not conjectural criticism dared?) we have at least the satisfaction of knowing, that no arbitrary departure from precedent and the only existing authorities could disturb the sense, or even tend to falsify the character of the writings of this great master. But substitutions of another sort do not only afford a shelter to ignorance and indolence; they rob the age of the testimony it gives of itself, they pollute the sources from which only the scholar can draw his materials to deduce the history of his native tongue, and deprive posterity of the means of ascertaining the characteristic features of the style of our great authors. Such must be the consequences of the wretched systems of some modern critics of at least no small pretensions; and such and no less are the sacrifices, they expect to be made to their petty studies and frivolous acquirements.

ABOUT a mile below Bidford, on the southern bank of the Avon, stands the village of Cleve, or Cliff, otherwise Cliff Priors. This place derives its name from a range of cliffs in its vicinity; and near to this spot we enter Worcestershire.

BENEATH these cliffs the Avon winds beautifully in a very spacious but shallow course: its bed is rocky, but perfectly level, and not more than four feet deep. Cleve mill, and lock, form a very picturesque scene; but the elevated rocky back ground renders the whole too confined to become a fit subject for the pencil.

WINDING round the cliff, the church of Salford breaks pleasingly on the view: here the Avon is joined by the river Arrewe, or Arrow,

Arrow, probably so called from the swiftness of its current. This river derives its source from the Licky Hill, near Bromsgrove, in Worcestershire, and, passing the town of Alcester, gives the name of Arrow to a village in its neighbourhood, near which the Marquis of Yarmouth has a handsome seat called Ragley. " Salford," says Dugdale, " had its name originally from a salt spring " that hath been there, as the inhabitants " doo observe, from the accesse of pigeons to " the place where it was, which is now " choaked up." At this place was formerly a seat belonging to Sir Simon Clark, Bart. a name that should not be forgotten in this country, as it is to him we owe much of that information handed down to us by Dugdale. Of a descendant of this gentleman we give the following anecdote as we received it:—About seventy years ago, a Sir Simon Clark, being a very young man, agreed with his comrades to commit a robbery, and actually did so. It was no Godshill adventure: the booty

booty they met with amounted only to a few shillings, with which they immediately went to a public house, and being there apprehended, confessed the fact without reserve. They were all convicted, and Sir Simon was condemned to be transported; and being sent to one of the West India islands, remained there many years, and till his death, having, in the interval of that event and the period at which he regained his liberty, acquired a very considerable fortune.

About two miles below Salford is Harvington Lock, and Weir, which has been repaired with some of the fragments, and it is said, even the statues from Evesham abbey. However, at the time they were inshrined this application might have been considered, though it would then have been a profane and sacrilegious abuse, we know that a Saint, who has been long thrown from his niche, and a King, as Mr. Burke says and knows, so soon as he is " hurled from his
" throne,"

"throne," command no very great degree of respect: when they can bestow blessings and pensions, no doubt they will be in better odour, whether the character of the age is that of chivalry or the most opposite. And, weighing in our minds the miserable uncertainty and strange vicissitudes of every thing sublunary, what is there of mortal origin so high and so sacred, that may not in afflux of time be converted to the basest uses? as our Shakspeare, speaking of Julius Cæsar, and he could have named no greater character, warns us:

"That earth, which kept the world in awe,
"May stop a hole t'expel the winter's flaw."

The scenery near Harvington is bounded on the south by a range of hills, which derive their name from the adjacent village of Littleton. Behind this village the Breedon hills form a beautiful undulating line, which, receding in due gradation, happily unites
itself

itself with the aerial distance. Below Harvington is the village of Offenham, which takes its name from Offa, King of the East Angles, who, with Kenred, King of the Mercians, gave to the abbey of Evesham seven Mansæ in this place. These sovereigns died monks at Rome. The remains of an extensive wall and battlements appear, from the bank of the Avon, to have formed the boundary of this place.

OFFENHAM was formerly the favourite retirement of the Abbots of Evesham; but of the nature of their luxuries at this place, we find no vestiges. After the Dissolution it came to Sir Edward Hoby, in the twenty-third of Elizabeth, and then to the Hazelwoods. The college of Christchurch, Oxford, now presents to the curacy.

A LITTLE below this village, it is said, there was antiently a bridge; the spot retains the name, but no traces of it appear. A little

A little below this place, a small brook, called the Fork, empties itself into the Avon. This stream rises upon one of the Cotswold hills, called Weston; and passing through Honeybourne and Bradfordston, finishes its course at this place. At the extremity of this reach of the river, Bengworth church, Dumbleton hills, &c. form a beautiful diversity of objects, considered as the back ground for a picture.

NEARLY on a line with what is called Offenham bridge, to the north of the village, stands a large rude stone, almost overgrown with ivy: its base is an oblong one foot nine inches by one foot two, rather diminishing towards the top; it has no traces of inscription or ornament, nor is there any marking of a chissel: it yet appears to have been placed there for some particular purpose; it stands between two hills, at about one hundred yards distant from the bank of the river, and on the north-west side of the field whereon the famous battle of Evesham was fought between the Barons and the King's forces in the reign of Henry the Third.

About a mile before we reach Evesham, the Avon receives the waters from Willersey, Broadway, and the adjacent hills, which running by Wickhamford, unite below Badsey, and under the name of Pludor Brook, falls into our river.

SECTION XI.

THE approach to Evesham presents an assemblage of objects happily combined for pictorial representation, although the most venerable remains of this antient place are concealed in the general view. The fertile vale of Evesham, besides its contiguity to our river, holds out so many invitations, and is a spot so peculiarly eligible to every class and description of men, who make it the study and business of their lives to bask in sunshine, indolence and plenty, that it is no wonder we should find hoods and cowls swarming and battening in this delicious and fruitful vale. Previous to the foundation of the abbey, Evesham was admired for its solitude. Upon this principle, no doubt, and that he might

might there undisturbed hold commerce with the skies, Egwin, the third Bishop of Worcester, applied to Ethelward, King of Mercia, for a grant of some wood lands in the neighbourhood, and obtained them. Monkish writers tell us the name of this place was derived from one Eoves, a swineherd to the Bishop, who, looking after a sow, which had strayed among the thickets, met the Virgin Mary in company with two other beautiful Virgins, each holding a pretty book and chaunting hymns. The report of this vision coming to the ears of the Bishop, zeal more than curiosity led him to the spot; when, as he began his orisons, he was indulged with the beatific vision, and was thereby encouraged to fulfil a vow he had formerly made to erect a church. For this pious purpose he obtained a grant from Kenred, King of Mercia, and Offa, son to the King of the East Angles, of sixty-
seven

seven manses of land, situated on the banks of the Avon. The King, the Prince and the Bishop soon after made a journey to the Pope Constantine, from whom they found no difficulty in obtaining a letter to summon to the spot where the beautiful virgins had so miraculously appeared, the Bishops, Sovereigns, and Nobles, from all parts of England, and declare before them, that Egwin had authority from the apostolic see, for founding there a monastery of Benedictines. Established with so much ceremony, and on this pious fraud the Abbey rapidly increased in wealth. The imagination of its holy founder, with some one or other of these delicious images that had hovered round him as he knelt in the field, caused the good Egwin to grow restless in any other place, to resign his see, and to become the first Abbot of his own foundation. Through his powerful and active patronage, we find it in the year 714 endowed with no less than twenty-two towns.

OTHER

OTHER accounts say, that the founder went to Rome, on account of the sins of his youth; that his legs were chained and fastened with an horse-lock, the key of which he had thrown into the sea; declaring that he would not be released till God by a miracle had declared the forgiveness of his sins; this story proceeds to state, that as he was returning to the English shore, a fish jumped into the boat, and that in its belly was found the key: others say he bought the fish at Rome, which, as it is making a fish a missionary, is no small improvement of the miracle. In confirmation of this wonderful story, the arms of the abbey are, according to Bishop Tanner's plate of Abbatial Seals, a horse-lock, or chain, which forms a chevron between three mitres. Another seal alludes to the adventure of the swineherd Eoves, who is represented in its centre surrounded by his herd. We shall here quit the absurd history of this once extensive foun-

foundation, and refer to its venerable ruins; which, dismissing from our minds that indignation which is so apt to rise at the many juggles and deceptions originally employed in too many of these establishments, cannot fail in their present state to interest the lover of antiquity, who may perhaps concur with the moralist in thinking, that these things produce a much better effect in decay and ruins, than in their pristine and most flourishing condition. In passing to these remains, the town of Evesham rises by an easy ascent from the bank of the Avon; which forms the peninsula on which it is situated. The town is healthy, and its soil celebrated for its fertility. The vale of Evesham, which takes its name from the town, Camden observes " is from its fruit-
" fulness styled the granary of these parts;
" so liberal is the soil in affording the best
" corn in great abundance."

THIS

This place is famed in history for the battle fought between the Barons and the royal forces in the reign of Henry the Third, in which the former, under the command of the Earl of Leicester, who married the King's sister, took prisoner the King, and his brother Richard, King of the Romans, and their two sons. The fatal cause of the battle, was the harsh reply received by the Barons from the King on their presenting petitions for the redress of their grievances; and this induced them to shake off their allegiance.

After the victory, the principal leaders having quarrelled among themselves, an army was formed under the command of Prince Edward, who made his escape from Hereford castle, and invested Evesham in August, 1265. He surrounded the Earl of Leicester's army, and forced him to battle in a large field about a mile to the north of the town. In this battle the Earl placed the captive King in the front,

front, in a suit of armour resembling his own: in which situation he was wounded in the shoulder, and would have been killed, had he not found means in time to discover himself to the soldiers. Leicester placed his barber on the abbey tower, as a spy, who, as soon as he saw the great strength of the Prince's army, cried out in despair, "Lord have "mercy on our souls, for our bodies are "theirs."—This battle terminated in the death of the Earl, and his eldest son Henry: the father fought on foot after his horse was killed, and was cut to pieces. The defeat of the Barons was immediately followed with the loss of the prime of the nobility, one hundred and sixty knights, many gentlemen, and about four thousand soldiers.

The bodies of the Earl and his son were buried in the abbey church before the altar, and the King is said to have assisted at their funeral.

Evesham was taken in May, 1644, by Maffey, and in July, Charles the Firft refreshed his foldiers here, and fent from hence propofals for peace to the Parliament at Weftminfter. In 1697, Evefham gave the title of Baron to Sir John Somers, Lord Chancellor of England, who was efteemed one of the ableft ftatefmen of his time.

Quitting Evefham a little below the bridge, the venerable remains of its once extenfive and magnificent abbey, with the churches of All Saints and St. Laurence, prefent themfelves in a very beautiful and picturefque point of view. The churches, although they appear connected in the annexed drawing, are feparate and diftinct buildings. The Abbot's tower is faid by Leland to have been built by Clement Litchfield, the laft Abbot but one; and in his Itinerary he quaintly remarks, that " He " made a right fumptuous and high fquare " tower

" towre of stone in the cemetary of Evesham.
" This towre had a great bell in it, and a
" goodly clocke, and was a gate house to one
" piece of the abbey." The great bell is
supposed to have been taken down at the
Restoration; when the young men of the
town joined together in the expence of melting down the bells of the two parish churches, and having that new set coined which are still hanging in the great tower. This venerable structure is one hundred and seventeen feet in height from its base, which is about twenty-two feet square, to the crown of the fanes. It is in a very chaste and elegant style of design: and its ornaments are simple, and perfectly beautiful. In all probability it was finished but a very short time before the Reformation, as it exhibits an admirable specimen of the improved taste of building at that period. It has suffered no dilapidation either from the hand of time, or the

more

more frantic one of religious or political zeal.

On the weſt front of this tower, above the dial, are two curious figures in wood, repreſenting men in armour. Their original employ was to ſtrike the hour; but they are now, from the ravage of time, become ſo ſtiff in their joints as to be no longer able to perform their functions. The figures appear to be the work of the middle of the laſt century. The date was originally inſcribed, but is now obliterated.

From the top of this noble tower, the admirer of extenſive views will be amply gratified with the beautiful ſcenery of the rich and fertile vale of Eveſham, and the ſurrounding country.

The ſite of the abbey, which ſtood to the left

left of the tower, is still distinctly marked by the ruins of its extensive walls; within which there are standing the beautiful remains of a chapel worthy the peculiar attention of the antiquary: its roofless walls, and broken windows, its mouldering arches, and beautiful appendage the clustering ivy, all leave a melancholy impression upon the mind, so far as it contemplates the instability of human labours and human institutions, at the same time that it is far from being overwhelmed with regret, when it reflects on the interested policy and unnatural restrictions of priestcraft, and of the church of Rome, once exhibited by its votaries within these walls. The site of the abbey is now occupied by Mr. Philips; at the extremity of whose garden, at the distance of about one hundred and fifty yards, facing the river, stands a venerable gateway, once the principal entrance to the abbey. The arch from the ground to the key stone is about seventeen feet high, but much

much of the effect of its height is lost by the falling in of rubbish from the adjoining ruins. The mouldings leave two ranges of niches, in which are sculptured in different compartments many figures of saints and monks, most of whom have lost their heads, in conformity perhaps to principles, in which, in stone and wood work at least, we seem here to have set the fashion to a neighbouring country. The draperies of some of them however display strong marks of excellence in their original design. The annexed view of this Gothic remain will give some idea of its present mutilated state, and of the charming village of Bengworth on the opposite side of the Avon, that was antiently among the many possessions of this wealthy abbey. Between the gate and the river were formerly their fish ponds; from whence they derived the means of using that singular species of ecclesiastical self-denial and fasting which at once satisfied the conscience and the appetite.

petite. From the end of the bridge, on the Evesham side, the remains of a wall are still visible, that formerly extended itself across the peninsula, and separated the fish ponds, gardens, and vineyard from the town. The extent and well chosen situation of these conveniencies indicate at once good taste in those spiritual directors, as well as a provident attention to those things that are necessary to our well being in this transitory state.

These charming grounds are watered by the gentle Avon, whose course brings us to the village of Hampton, about a mile below Evesham. This small village is beautifully situated on an eminence, embosomed within a rich thicket of oaks, and commands an extensive prospect of the luxuriant vale of Evesham. Here the Avon receives the aid of a small brook called the Vincell, that has its rise in the vicinity of Sudely Castle, in Gloucestershire, and, coming down by Winchcomb,

Winchcomb, and Todington, the seat of Lord Tracy, enters this county at Sedgbarow. The remain of the garden wall, antiently belonging to the abbey, extends a considerable distance along the margin of the river, and at the termination of this wall, a fine sloping bank verges upon the river for near a mile, exhibiting a rich display of fruit trees, planted with great regularity, and which seem to vie with the luxuriant vines of France and Italy. Every part of this charming vale is so abundantly fertile in fruit and garden productions of every kind as to supply the greater part of the neighbourhood. The sudden windings of the Avon, both here and below, render the distance twice as great by water as by land. Here also it increases very much in width, and its depth is fourteen or fifteen feet at least; and yet so inconsiderable is the traffic upon it, that not more than two barges go up in the course of a week to Evesham, and frequently not more than one

in

in a fortnight so high as Stratford. The great reduction of commerce on this river has been occasioned in no small degree by the Coventry and other canals in its vicinage.

The country, as we pass down, is finely screened by the Fladbury hills below, which, with Chatbury mill, and lock, and the surrounding scenery, combine so rich a landscape, that nature seems not to require the assistance of art, in the language of modern refinement, either to correct her coarse expression by removing a hill or docking a tree, or to supply her careless and tasteless omissions for the purpose of rendering her more completely picturesque.

Approaching Fladbury, we pass a handsome house on an eminence, the seat of the Perrots, and a few years since of George Perrot, Esq. late one of the Barons of the Exchequer, who purchased this manor, together

gether with the navigation of the river Avon, at this place.

HAVING in a former section observed that this river was made navigable in 1635 by a Mr. William Sandys, we feel it a duty again to mention so great a friend to our river, more especially as he was at the time a resident, and bailiff, in the parish of Fladbury. Dr. Nash, in his Worcestershire, page 447, quotes from an account of the water works of Mr. William Sandys, of Fladbury, " That he erected Wears in the " quietest streams. Nor did he intend to " finish his work at Stratford, but had " thoughts to extend the same to Warwick; " but what hindered his accomplishing his " design, I know not; and for the expence " he hath hereupon bestowed, it cannot be " reckoned less than twenty thousand pounds. From the same account it appears that " as " soon as he had finished his work to Stratford " (and,

" (and, as I have heard, spent all his fortune),
" he immediately delivered up all to the
" Parliament to do what more they thought
" fit therein."

The country about Fladbury is remarked for its fertility; a quality which the women in the neighbourhood are said to possess in a degree and at a period of life scarce elsewhere known, it being no uncommon circumstance, as I am informed, for women to bear children when advanced to near the age of sixty. Fladbury church contains some monuments worthy attention, particularly those of the antient and once eminent family of the Throckmortons. Its situation is well disposed for the picturesque, but is too much incumbered with trees tortured in the true Dutch style, to be worthy the pencil. The adjoining parsonage house may likewise be truly said to

" O'ertop

"O'ertop the houſe of God."

This, in a ſingle inſtance, reverſes the remark made by the incomparable Butler, however true it may be in other reſpects, "that "churchmen overlook all other people as "haughtily as the churches and ſteeples do "private houſes."

The village of Cropthorn, about a mile below, preſents a ſcene more noble and intereſting; the varying and capricious hand of faſhion in gardening has not interfered, and nature remains in that primitive ſtate of ſimplicity that conſtitutes at once the ſublime and beautiful in Engliſh landſcape. In the church of Cropthorn are two antient monuments of the Dineley family, who held conſiderable poſſeſſions in this vicinity for ſeveral centuries, and flouriſhed in this country with great repute till the beginning of the preſent; when, on the death of Sir Edward Dineley,

Dineley, his daughter and heir, Eleanor, married Edward Goodyere, of Burghope, in Herefordshire, who, in 1707, was created a Baronet. This gentleman was succeeded by his eldest son Sir John Dineley Goodyere, who was the last of the family that enjoyed this estate. He was so much at variance with his younger brother, Samuel Dineley Goodyere (Captain of the Ruby man of war), as to threaten to disinherit him in favour of his sister's son John Foote, of Truro, in Cornwall, Esq. This so irritated his brother, the Captain, that he took the desperate resolution of murdering the Baronet, and perpetrated it on the 17th of January, 1741. The circumstance is thus related by Dr. Nash, in his Worcestershire, p. 272: " A
" friend at Bristol, who knew their mortal
" antipathy, had invited them both to din-
" ner, in hopes of reconciling them, and
" they parted in seeming friendship; but
" the

" the Captain placed some of his crew in the
" street near College Green, with orders to
" seize his brother, and assisted in hurrying
" him by violence to his ship, under pretence
" that he was disordered in his senses, where,
" when they arrived, he caused him to be
" strangled in the cabin by White and
" Mahony, two ruffians of his crew, himself
" standing centinel at the door while the
" horrid deed was perpetrating. It is suffi-
" cient to say that the murder was immedi-
" ately discovered, and the Captain and his
" two accomplices being tried at Bristol
" March 26th following, were found guilty,
" and there executed, April 15th. The
" Captain had behaved bravely in his pro-
" fession on several occasions; was at the
" taking of St. Sebastian, Ferrol, and St.
" Antonio, at which latter place he burnt
" three men of war, the magazine, and
" stores." The heir to the estate was John
Foote,

Foote, Efq. nephew to Sir John, and elder brother to the late Samuel Foote, Efq. our celebrated comedian.

BELOW Cropthorn, at the village of Piddle, and near the bridge, the Avon receives the waters that come down from Breedon hill and from Elmely caftle. After paffing the extenfive meadows of Fladbury, they unite with feveral brooks from the north, and empty themfelves into our river at this fpot.

FROM thefe acceffions our Avon acquires a confiderable breadth, and aided by a richly diverfified fcenery, comprifing a diftant view of Perfhore, yields to the eye, in paffing down the ftream, a moft beautiful and luxuriant landfcape.

SECTION XII.

PERSHORE, once famed for its abbey and extensive church possessions, is now not less so for the beauty of its situation and fertility of its soil. It stands on the northern bank of our Avon, from which it derives its principal advantage; and, together with great improvements in its adjoining roads, has, within the last few years increased greatly in population. Its name, Camden tells us, is derived from a Saxon word, which signifies a Pear Tree. The pear tree is certainly to be found here in great abundance; but we much doubt the fact of its name originating from that tree, as that fruit was not produced in England till about the middle of the sixteenth century, at which period both cherries and grapes were likewise introduced.

On the reduction of the Papal power in this country, Perfhore appears to have loft its former confequence. The abbey of Perfhore, according to William of Malmfbury, bears date as early as 604: after which period, having received various orders of religious perfons and having been feveral times deftroyed by fire, it at length fell into the hands of a more powerful body, the Monks of Weftminfter. In the laft fire in 1287 it is faid, that the regifter of the eftates, with the cuftoms and charters of the abbey, was deftroyed; and that Walter, the then Prior, and others being examined touching their privileges, fome demands of a very curious nature were brought forward—claims that would even ftartle the confcience of the moft rapacious modern ecclefiaftic. Among others this was infifted upon by the Prior, that the principal legacy, bequeathed by every deceafed perfon within their parifhes, ought to be carried before the corpfe to the church of Perfhore, shore, and there valued by the Sacrist and Chaplain of the place to which the deceased belonged; and that one half of the valuation should remain with the Sacrist, and the other be given to the chaplain. This pious custom requires no other comment than that, when it first obtained, it must have originated in fraud, and so long as it continued, was a barefaced robbery.

Of this once extensive abbey, the site of which contained about two acres, we find very small remains, no more than the tower, the southern part of the cross, and one of its chapels. At the Dissolution, it was valued, according to Speed, at six hundred and sixty-six pounds thirteen shillings.

In the 11th of the reign of Henry the Third, he granted to the Abbot and Monks of this place a fair to be held, on the feast of St. Edburgh of Pershore, in the church-yard of Holy Cross. St. Edburgh was the eighth daughter of King Edward the Elder, who reigned in 901. This pious lady, we are told, was from her infancy much inclined to godly books and good works; and that her father, as a test, and to prove her zeal genuine, frequently placed before her fine clothes and rich jewels on the one hand, and on the other the New Testament and other devout tracts: and that such was her constancy, that she uniformly rejected the finery, and made choice of the implements of devotion. In return for her indifference to the pomps and vanities of this world, it is added, she was placed in a monastery at Winchester; where we only know that she died and was buried. Few of the Misses of the present day would have made such a choice, and still fewer would have approved the mode of rewarding it; they dwell with little satisfaction upon the idea of " single blessed-" ness;" but cannot at all apprehend the notion of being spouses of the Lord.

We

WE have before observed in the course of this work, that fairs were originally held to solemnize the feast of the dedication of churches, and that they were then kept within the churches; but in the above reign, on account of the irregularities practised on those occasions, a special mandate was issued to forbid their being there kept: and the fair at this place was appointed to be held in the church-yard. These irregularities are strongly pointed at in a black letter book published in 1493, in a dialogue between Dives and Pauper. It runs thus:

" *Dives.* What sayest thou of them
" that hold markets and feyers in holy
" church and sanctuary?

" *Pauper.* Both the buyer and the seller
" and the men of holy church; that maintain
" them, or suffer them, when they might let
" it, been accursed. They make Goddes
" house

" house a den of thieves; for commonly in
" such feyres and markets, wheresoever it be
" holden, there be many thieves, mychers,
" and cut purses.

" *Dives.* And I dread me, that full
" often by such feyres Goddes house is made
" a tavern of gluttons, and a bordel of ly-
" chors; for the merchant and chapman
" keep their wives and lemans both night
" and day; and what if the prelates and
" curates of the place take money of the
" chapmen for the place that they stand
" in by covenant?"

This last is a sarcastic query; but as the glebe of holy church in these days is never suffered to pass into lay hands without a consideration made, why in this case should an agistment tithe be thought unreasonable? To be sure, if they took no tithe in kind, under the circumstances of a commerce so

promis-

promiscuous, in which many a holy father might chance to pick up a new toy, there must at least have been laid in a rich harvest of sins against the day of confession: on which occasion we will charitably hope, that forgiveness of a first lapse was never purchased by a confirmation in evil.

In the abbey church are some antient monuments; and amongst them is preserved the inscription of Abbot Newton, or Newnton, who built the south cross aisle. It is given in a rebus, in which the name is inserted above a tun; thus mixing hieroglyphic with their description—a mode of conveying their meaning by no means unusual in those times.

In the vicinity of Pershore, the Avon has a greater depth and breadth of water than we have yet witnessed; and the general landscape, as we approach the foot of Bredon hill,

hill, combines likewise a highly improved scene of vegetation. The view is rendered still more pleasing by an extensive woody scenery that presents itself on a rising bank of the river.

PASSING the village of Cumberton, Malvern hills, in a grey sombre tint, form a pleasing back ground to a rich thicket of oaks, that borders the southern bank of the river. This scenery receives no small pictorial aid from the adjoining lock and mill; that take their name from the village of Nafford, which is bounded on the west by Eckington. Here a handsome bridge of six irregular arches is thrown across the Avon, it is built of that reddish stone so generally produced in this country. The road over this bridge leads from Pershore to Tewksbury.

A LITTLE below this spot the Avon receives

ceives a further acceffion from a fmall ftream called Dufford, or, as it was antiently written, Depeford brook. In this neighbourhood is found a weak brine, that has been frequently worked, but never to much advantage.

At a fudden bend of the river, Strenfham church appears on a confiderable eminence. This building, on a nearer approach, affords, with the furrounding objects and the beautiful mill beneath on the bank of the Avon, a fcene which equally invites the pencil of the artift, and the pen of the obfervant traveller. This village has, befides its peculiarly pleafing fituation, a yet ftronger claim to notice from having produced that extraordinary and, in his line, unrivalled genius, Samuel Butler, author of Hudibras. He was born in 1612, and on the eighth day of February following was baptifed in the parifh church of Strenfham. The font at which he was baptised is yet standing; it is of stone, and the style of its workmanship leaves no room to doubt that it is of a date more antient than the birth of our unrivalled wit. It appears that the father of Butler was churchwarden of this place the year before our author was born, and that he occupied a considerable farm of about three hundred pounds a year, which he rented of Sir William Russel, then Lord of the manor of Strensham, besides a small tenement and lands, his own property, of the annual value at that time of eight pounds. In these premises, which are now divided into three tenements, our author is said to have been born; and they still retain the appellation of Butler's tenements. Although some doubts have arisen respecting this fact, I am yet inclined to give credit to it; and am strengthened in this persuasion by the concurrence of the Reverend Dr. Nash of Bevereye, near Worcester; who is the present Lord of the manor, and, together with

with the other Ruffel eftates, owner of thefe premifes.

In the preceding wood cut I have preserved a faithful fketch of the humble retreat of this very original genius. Nor fhould the high and original character of his wit be confidered as the only great and diftinguifhing feature of Butler's mufe: his profound and various learning, and his inexhauftible treafure of univerfal knowledge appear to lay equal claim to our applaufe and admiration.

tion. Dennis, in the following lines inscribed on his monument in Westminster abbey, has most happily given a true idea of the character of the genius of this very superior man:

> "He was a whole species of poets in one;
> "Admirable in a manner
> "In which no one else has been tolerable:
> "A manner which begun and ended in him,
> "In which he knew no guide,
> "And has found no followers."

WITH the lands possessed by Dr. Nash, formerly in the hands of Butler's family, he holds, if not a treasure of inestimable value, a work of very great curiosity and interest—the common place book of our author.

I WAS gratified by the Doctor with a sight of this repository, in which is lodged a series of those passages in contemporary writers, the force of which impressed them upon the understanding, or the brilliancy of which struck

struck the warm and vivid imagination of our masculine wit: and I have no doubt but that a correct copy of it, given to the public, would prove highly interesting to the philosophic and reflecting mind, that delights to follow genius in its retirement, and compare the nature of its private studies and pursuits with the character of its known and avowed labours and occupations, and to know the turn of thought that would recommend itself to an intellect of so much vigour, and a wit so truly original. It would probably also be acceptable to the antiquary, and assuredly to the less solemn trifler, the collector of the curiosities of literature.

THE extreme indigence in which Butler notoriously died, would of itself have been a reproach to the literary character of the age: but without derogating from the high estimation to which he is entitled, we cannot forget that either their envy or their selfish diffi-

diffipation fuffered "one greater" to defcend to the grave almoft a beggar. Whatever excufe might be at hand for the neglect of Milton in this quarter, it muft remain an eternal ftigma upon the character of ariftocracy, that fo uniform, fo refolute, and active a fupporter of fupremacies fhould have died a fans culottes. As to the Monarch, it was not poffible that any thing could add to his exceeding infamy. His unhappy fate is lamented by the ingenious Mr. Samuel Wefley of Tiverton, in the following epigrammatic epitaph, written in confequence of a buft having been erected in honour of his memory:

"When Butler, needy wretch, was yet alive,
"No generous patron would a dinner give.
"See him now lifelefs and reduced to duft
"Prefented with a monumental buft.
"The poet's fate is here in emblem fhewn;
"He afk'd for bread and he receiv'd a ftone."

WITHIN

Within the church of Strenſham are ſome well executed monuments of the Ruſſel family, who flouriſhed in this place upwards of four hundred years. A Sir William Ruſſel of Strenſham during the civil wars ſuffered greatly from his adherence to the royal cauſe, and expended large ſums in the King's ſervice; and yet, after the Reſtoration took place, and the order of the royal oak was about to be inſtituted, his eſtate was valued at eight thouſand pounds a year.

Quitting Strenſham we paſs Bredon, the name of which has been obſerved to ſignify a place at the root of a hill, from the word Braidd, extremity, and Don, a hill.

The rectory houſe is pleaſantly ſituated on a riſing eminence on the bank of the river, and ſeems to cover much more ground than the houſe of God; the porch and weſt end of which are in the Saxon ſtyle of architecture. The rectory is one of of the most valuable in the diocese of Worcester.

We cannot quit this village without mentioning the name of Dr. Prideaux, formerly Bishop of Worcester; who, upon the sequestration of his bishopric during the civil wars, retired hither on a stipend of only four shillings and sixpence per week. This reverse of fortune he bore with much chearfulness, although obliged to sell his books and furniture to procure subsistence. One day being asked by a neighbour as he passed through the village with something under his gown, What he had got there? He replied he was become an ostrich, and forced to live upon iron; shewing some old iron which he was going to sell at the blacksmiths to enable himself to purchase a dinner.

Below Bredon, at Twinings Fleet, which is about three miles before you reach Tewksbury, the tower of that church and the surrounding

rounding objects form a very pleasing distance; but it being near the close of the day when we saw it, the whole appeared too misty and indistinct for the pencil and size of this work. Twinings Fleet takes its name from the parish of Twining, which is situate on a point of land north-west of the Avon, and is between that and the Severn.

NEAR the village is the remain of a considerable encampment, said to be Roman; of which I shall treat more at large in the History of the Severn, as from its contiguity it more properly belongs to that river.

BEFORE we reach Tewkfbury, our Avon receives considerable aid from the river Carrant, which rises in Beckford, and is a boundary between the counties of Worcester and Gloucester.

APPROACHING Mythe bridge, the antient

tient tower of the abbey church of Tewkſbury, and other objects, pleaſingly combine in the general landſcape of this venerable place; and we cannot ſelect, towards the concluſion of this work, a more proper object than a repreſentation of that ſpot,

" Where Avon's friendly ſtreams with Severn join,
" And Tewkſbury's walls, renown'd for trophies, ſhine."

Mythe bridge was built in 1632; and this ſtructure conſtitutes a part of what is called the long bridge. Previous to the period of building this bridge, the old one meaſured above ſeven hundred yards in length. A bridge of this extent became neceſſary from the frequent floods that happen in the long level of this country. The greateſt ever remembered took place in 1770: it was occaſioned by a very heavy fall of ſnow, ſucceeded by rain that continued for three days; during which time large boats with twelve or fourteen

teen people paſſed and repaſſed the town to ſupply the inhabitants with neceſſaries. The next year the tide flowed in Avon five inches perpendicular, a circumſtance never before on record. Mythe bridge derives its name from a hamlet belonging to Tewkſbury, called the Mythe, a word of Greek derivation, which ſignifies a military ſtation. For this purpoſe it is happily formed by nature, being difficult of acceſs in every part, and receiving additional ſecurity from the confluence of the Severn and Avon in the valley beneath.

The ſummit of the hill, or Tumulus at this beautiful place, formerly bore the name of the Mythe Toot; but ſince it received a royal viſit in the year 1788, it has changed its name to Royal Hill.

Tewksbury, although it may properly be conſidered as appertaining to our preſent purſuit, purfuit, being on the bank of what is called the Old Avon, is yet an object, we conceive, better fuited to the more extenfive and impetuous Severn, than to the gentle and foft flowing Avon. We fhall therefore fufpend any remark on that refpectable and antient town till the Hiftory of the river Severn is laid before the public. In the interim we beg to fubmit, with all due refpect, as fome return for our want of ability to render juftice to the beauties of the prefent fubject, the fidelity and attention with which the views were made, and the earneft and unremitted diligence ufed in procuring the information contained in this volume.

FINIS.

www.ingramcontent.com/pod-product-compliance
Lightning Source LLC
Chambersburg PA
CBHW031328230426
43670CB00006B/273